SEIZE
THE DAY

SEIZE
THE DAY

Living on Purpose and Making
Every Day Count

JOYCE MEYER

NEW YORK · NASHVILLE

FaithWords
Hachette Book Group
1290 Avenue of the Americas
New York, NY 10104
faithwords.com
twitter.com/faithwords

First published in hardcover by Center Street in September 2016
First Trade Paperback Edition: October 2017

FaithWords is a division of Hachette Book Group, Inc.
The FaithWords name and logo are trademarks of Hachette Book Group, Inc.

The publisher is not responsible for websites (or their content) that are not owned by the publisher.

The Hachette Speakers Bureau provides a wide range of authors for speaking events. To find out more, go to www.hachettespeakersbureau.com or call (866) 376-6591.

Unless otherwise noted Scripture quotations are taken from *The Amplified Bible* (Amplified ® Bible), Copyright © 1954, 1958, 1962, 1964, 1965, 1987 by The Lockman Foundation Used by permission. (www.Lockman.org)

Scriptures noted (THE MESSAGE) are taken from *The Message: The Prophets* by Eugene Peterson. Copyright © 2000 by Eugene H. Peterson. NavPress Publishing Group, P.O. Box 35001, Colorado Springs, CO 80935. Used by permission.

Scriptures noted (NIV) are taken from the *Holy Bible: New International Version®*. Copyright © 1973, 1978, 1984 by International Bible Society. Used by permission of Zondervan Publishing House. All rights reserved.

Scripture quotations marked (NKJV) are taken from the *New King James Version*. Copyright © 1979, 1980, 1982 by Thomas Nelson, Inc., Publishers.

Scriptures noted (TLB) are taken from *The Living Bible*, Copyright © 1971. Used by permission of Tyndale House Publishers, Inc., Wheaton, Illinois 60189. All rights reserved.

Scripture quotations marked (NLT) are taken from the *Holy Bible*, New Living Translation, Copyright © 1996. Used by permission of Tyndale House Publishers, Inc., Wheaton, Illinois 60189. All rights reserved.

Scripture quotations marked (GNT) are taken from the *Good News Translation—Second Edition*, Copyright © 1992, by the American Bible Society. Used by permission. All rights reserved.

Scriptures noted (CEV) are taken from the *Contemporary English Version*, Copyright © 1995 by the American Bible Society. Used by permission.

Library of Congress Cataloging-in-Publication Data has been applied for.

ISBNs: 978-1-4555-5994-7 (trade paperback), 978-1-4555-5989-3 (hardcover), 978-1-4555-5990-9 (large print), 978-1-4555-5991-6 (ebook), 978-1-4555-9832-8 (international), 978-1-4789-4530-7 (international / South African)

Printed in the United States of America

LSC-C

10 9 8 7 6 5 4

CONTENTS

Recently I realized that I have already lived more of my life than what I have left, and somehow that made me even more determined than ever to make the most of my time. I think when we get past the age of fifty or sixty, we begin to think quite differently about our life and what we want to do with our time than we did perhaps when we were twenty, thirty, or even forty. We realize more clearly how precious time is, and in my case (and I hope in yours), we want to make sure that we don't waste any of it.

Do you ever have plans for the day and then get to the end of it and feel frustrated and perhaps even a bit angry with yourself? You had a plan that seemed good, but you didn't do much of what you planned to do, and, to be honest, you are not real sure what you did do. You were busy all day, but you only remember doing fragmented pieces of things depending on whatever seemed the most urgent at the time. Actually, when you think about it, you must admit you don't recall finishing anything significant.

Your plan was to pay the bills, go to the grocery store, get the oil changed in your car, and cook a nice dinner for your family. You really wanted to do the dinner because just last week one of your teenagers said, "Mom, why don't we ever all sit down to eat dinner together like we did when I was little?" You didn't have an answer because you're not sure what the reason is. It just seems that life is so busy that having dinner together never happens!

Is it hard for you to focus on what you really want and need to do because of all the interruptions you deal with all day? Have your e-mail, Facebook, and Twitter accounts made your life easier or just busier? All of the modern conveniences can, of course, be very good, but only if we manage them and avoid letting the buzzes, dings, and beeps they make control us.

Are you steadily becoming the person you really want to be? Are you accomplishing the things you want to accomplish in life? Are you an "on-purpose" person, or do you drift through the days, weeks, months, and years waiting to see where life takes you? Do you need to take charge of your life? Is it time for a change? Do you need to seize the day today and every day?

I am usually a very goal-oriented individual, and I am motivated by accomplishment so I stay on track, but in the past year I found myself looking at the piles of things I needed and wanted to do and becoming so double-minded about which one to do first that I often ended up doing nothing, or at best just doing little bits and pieces of several things, none of which I finished. Oh, I finished the things I absolutely had to do, but, to be honest, I was wasting a lot of precious time and feeling aggravated at myself because I seemed to spend more time trying to figure out what to do than I did doing anything. I felt really overwhelmed and that is unusual for me, so I really started praying about it and wanted to hear what God would say to me about the situation. I felt life was ordering me around rather than me ordering my life, and I knew something was wrong.

As I prayed about it, God began showing me the importance of living life "on purpose"—something I had done most of my life but had somehow gotten off track. I think part of the reason why I encountered the season of passivity and double-mindedness was so I would feel an urgency to write this book. As I started listening to people, I found that a large percentage live their lives day in and day out without accomplishing much of what they truly intended to. They were busy, but not sure what they were busy with. "I'm busy" has become the standard excuse for all the things we should have done but didn't do. If you see a friend you used to hear from regularly but now cannot get him or her to return your calls, he or she will assuredly say, "I'm sorry I haven't called you back; I have just been very busy." We recently waited almost three weeks to secure an appointment for a carpet bid. When we called the salesman for the third time, he said, "I'm sorry it has taken me so long to get back to you—we have just been so busy!" What if God never answered our calls and then gave the excuse of being too busy?

I truly wonder how many people at the end of their life feel they lived the life they were meant to live. How many have only regrets about the things they did or did not do during their life? You only have one life, and if it is not going in the direction you want it to, now is the time to make changes.

When we live unproductive lives, we should not blame it on circumstances, other people, the way the world is today, or anything else. God created man and gave him free will. That means we have the ability to make choices in literally every area of life, and if we don't make our own choices guided by God, we will end up with nothing but regrets.

God has a will and purpose for each of us, and His desire is that we use our free will to choose His will so we can enjoy the best life possible. I hope and pray that as you read this book you will learn to "seize the day" and start making the moments you have count toward fulfilling your potential!

This book is about learning to live life "on purpose," therefore, I will be suggesting a lot of things you need to "do" or "not do" in order to make that goal a reality. However, it is very important to me that I don't leave anyone with the impression that God's love for us, or our right standing with Him, is the result of anything we *do*. That is "works"-oriented religion and is not what God offers us through Jesus Christ. I think the best way to make my point is by using the book of Ephesians in the Bible.

Ephesians is broken into six chapters. The first three chapters are all about how much God loves us, and it teaches us that His love is a free gift that is given unconditionally. Paul writes that while we were dead in sin, God made us alive in Christ, offering us a brand-new life, and He raised us up with Him, inviting us to enter His rest. He did all of this before we ever knew Him or even cared to know Him. Grace—amazing grace—provided everything!

Ephesians makes it clear that our salvation is not based on our works or anything that we could ever do. It is a free gift of God! Salvation is free! Mercy is free! The forgiveness of our sins is free! Although it is free to us, it was costly for Jesus. He gave His life, shedding His blood in order for us to enjoy relationship with God through Him.

For it is by free grace (God's unmerited favor) that you are saved (delivered from judgment and made partakers of

Christ's salvation) through [your] faith. And this [salvation]
is not of yourselves [of your own doing; it came not through
your own striving], but it is the gift of God;
   Not because of works [not the fulfillment of the Law's
demands], lest any man should boast. [It is not the result of
what anyone can possibly do, so no one can pride himself in it
or take glory to himself.]

Ephesians 2:8–9

Our right standing with God is a gift of God's grace that is
received only by faith and not by works or anything we can ever do.

However, beginning in Ephesians chapter 4, and continuing
through chapter 6, the apostle Paul instructs the believers in
the behavior they should have in light of what God has done for
them. He mentions many things that will require choices, and he
urges us to make the right ones.

The good things that we choose to do should always be done
because God loves us and because we love Him, and never with the
thought that we can "earn" or "buy" His love by doing them. Let
me be clear that we do not earn salvation or the love of God; however, there are rewards for us here on earth (and in eternity) that
are based on what we do while in the body. God doesn't want us
to miss out on them, and we should not want to, either. Our right
relationship with God should always provoke obedience, and that
obedience leads us into a life that is truly amazing.

I am urging you today to live the best life you possibly can for
the glory of God as a way of honoring Him and thanking Him for
what He has done for you. I frequently teach on behavior, but all
good behavior must be rooted in the foundation of our relationship with God through Christ if it is to have any real value.

Anytime we are struggling with "doing" the right thing, we

should *not* just try harder! We should abide in God's love, returning to the scriptures time and again that teach us about the love of God! Ask for God's help, and let Him strengthen you for what you need to do. The more you realize how perfectly God loves you, the more you will have a desire to do all He asks you to do.

CHAPTER 1

Man's Free Will

I have set before you life and death, the blessing and the curse; therefore, you shall choose life in order that you may live, you and your descendants.

Deuteronomy 30:19

In order to seize the day and live the life God wants us to live, it is vital that we understand man's free will. God created man with free will and His desire was (and still is) that man would use that free will to choose *His* will. God promises to guide those who are willing to do His will (see John 7:17). It will be difficult to understand the message of this book unless we are

> Free will is a huge responsibility as well as a privilege and a freedom.

willing to understand we are creatures with a free will and we are responsible for the choices we make. Free will is a huge responsibility as well as a privilege and a freedom. God will always guide us to make the choices that will work best for us and lead us into His plan for us, but He will never force or manipulate us into making that choice.

Each day that God gives us is definitely a gift, and we have an opportunity to value it. One of the ways to do that is to use each day purposefully, not wasting time or allowing ourselves to be manipulated by circumstances that we cannot control. Each day can count if we learn to live it "on purpose" rather than passively drifting through the day, allowing the wind of circumstances and distractions to make our choices for us. We can remember at all times that we are God's children and He has created us to rule our days, directing each one into His purpose for our lives. In the beginning of time, God gave man dominion and told him to be fruitful and multiply and use the resources he had in the service of God and man. It sounds to me as if God told Adam to "Seize the day!"

C. S. Lewis said this about man's free will:

> God created things which had free will. That means creatures which can go wrong or right. Some people think they can imagine a creature which was free but had no possibility of going wrong, but I can't. If a thing is free to be good it's also free to be bad. And free will is what has made evil possible. Why, then, did God give them free will? Because free will, though it makes evil possible, is also the only thing that makes possible any love or goodness or joy worth having. A world of automata—of creatures that worked like machines— would hardly be worth creating. The happiness which God designs for His higher creatures is the happiness of being freely, voluntarily united to Him and to each other in an ecstasy of love and delight compared with which the most rapturous love between a man and a woman on this earth is mere milk and water. And for that they've got to be free.
>
> Of course God knew what would happen if they used their freedom the wrong way: apparently, He thought it worth the risk....If God thinks this state of war in the

universe a price worth paying for free will—that is, for making a real world in which creatures can do real good or harm and something of real importance can happen, instead of a toy world which only moves when He pulls the strings—then we may take it it is worth paying.[1]

God gave us free will and, if we intend to use it for God's purposes, we will pay a price to do so, but, as C. S. Lewis said, "It is worth paying." We pay a price not only to do the right thing, but we also pay a price if we do the wrong thing. I submit to you that the price we pay for wrong choices is much greater and leaves us sorrowful and filled with regret and misery.

I watched my mom and dad make wrong choices most of their lives, and I also watched them pay the price for those choices. My dad chose anger, alcohol, and a life without God. During most of his life, he chose to fulfill his sexual desires at a high cost to others. He sexually abused me, as well as several other people, for many years. He was regularly unfaithful to my mother, as well as violent, and she passively stood by and made excuses for not taking action to protect herself or my brother and me. Although I am happy to say they both died believing in God and having repented of their sins, I must also say they missed the good life God had planned for them, and they both ended life filled with regret for the choices they had made.

They did not make right choices because, in both of their cases, it would have required setting aside their feelings and trusting God to help them overcome their weaknesses. My father had a sexual addiction, and my mother was filled with fear. I am quite sure you could think of several people you know who are currently making wrong choices simply because they would find it difficult to do the right thing, or they are deceived into thinking that their wrong choices will make them happy. It is absolutely astounding how many people destroy their lives because they are unwilling to do difficult things. "It is too hard" is one of the biggest excuses I hear when I encourage people to change their life by changing their choices to ones that agree with God's will.

You and I can choose what we will do each day. We choose our thoughts, words, attitudes, and behaviors. We cannot always choose what our circumstances will be, but we can choose how we will respond to them. We are free agents! When we use our freedom to choose to do the will of God, He is honored and glorified. We can choose to make each day count—to accomplish something worthwhile—or we can choose to waste the day.

In his book *The Secret of Guidance*, F. B. Meyer said, "Perhaps you live too much in your feelings and too little in your will. We have no direct control over our feelings, but we have over our will. Our wills are ours, to make them God's. God does not hold us responsible for what we feel, but for what we will. In His sight we are not what we feel, but what we will. Let us, therefore, not live in the summerhouse of emotion, but in the central citadel of the will, wholly yielded and devoted to the will of God."[2]

Most of us know people who live entirely by their feelings, and the result is that they are wasting their lives. But that can change quickly if they will make a different decision, one that is in agreement with God's will.

One of my grandsons chose to move away from home at age eighteen, and for the next year he stayed drunk daily and took drugs regularly. He didn't work, and he lived in an apartment with several other young men who were on the same path, one of whom died from a drug overdose. For that year he lived completely according to his emotions. Thankfully, he realized he was going in a wrong direction, and he chose to call his parents and ask if he could come back home. Within a few months he was restored, free from alcohol and drugs, and was busy developing a relationship with God. He is now working in ministry, married to a lovely Christian young woman, and raising his children.

He chose the wrong path and then, thankfully, he chose the right path. It is wonderful to realize that with God's help, we can correct mistakes we've made. When we make wrong choices, we always reap the result of them sooner or later, and it is never pleasant. Reaping what we sow is a spiritual law that God has put into place in the universe, and it works the same way every time. If we sow to the flesh, we reap from the flesh ruin, decay, and destruction. But if we sow to the Spirit, we reap life (see Galatians 6:8). No matter how much bad seed (self-will and disobedience) anyone has planted, the moment they begin to plant good seed (obedience to God), their lives will begin to change for the better. God's mercy is new every morning—that means He has provided a way for us to begin fresh each day!

God's Grace

God's grace is His undeserved favor and His enabling power. Grace is manifested when God does good things for us that we don't deserve. When we sin, we can repent and ask for God's forgiveness and, thankfully, His grace provides it freely.

When we choose to do God's will, our intent is right, but we may still need help following through and doing what we have chosen to do. It is God's grace that provides that help through the Holy Spirit. Often the thing God asks of us is something we find to be difficult to do without assistance, but with God all things are possible (see Matthew 19:26). Not asking God for help is the underlying cause of most failure. Do you regularly ask the Holy

Spirit, Who is your Helper, to help you? If you have not known to do so, you will see amazing changes in your life as you simply ask.

If I am very angry at my husband and have no desire to forgive him but I know from my study of God's Word and the conviction of the Holy Spirit that I need to choose to forgive no matter how I feel, I ask God to help me do the good thing I want to do. I choose, and God provides the grace (power) for me to do it. I had to fail many times in order to learn that I could not do it on my own. God desires that we be dependent upon Him, not independent from Him.

> God desires that we be dependent upon Him, not independent from Him.

God gives us free will, and we can make right or wrong choices. Each of them carries with it a harvest that we will reap, for God's Word clearly states that we will reap what we sow. Yet, even if we do choose God's will, we will still need His help in following through. It is easy to decide on Sunday evening after dinner that you are going on a diet starting Monday morning, but can you follow through on Monday evening when you are at a restaurant and they bring out the dessert tray? That is often when we need God's help!

Jesus came filled with grace and truth (see John 1:17). He reveals truth to us and then gives us grace to walk in it if it is our choice to do so.

God's Sovereignty

Many people find it very difficult to reconcile God's sovereignty and man's free will. It is not anything we need to be confused about. Very simply put: we are partners with God. He works in and through us to help us accomplish His will. When He finds someone who will choose His will and allow Him to work through them, that person becomes a light in a dark world, or an example of what life with God can be like. The person can be used by God to encourage others also to choose God and His ways.

If we have no freedom of choice, then we are merely puppets, with God pulling the strings. Our love for God is meaningless unless we are giving it freely.

This is what Andrew Murray said about human will:[3]

> The human will is the power by which a person determines his actions, and decides what to do or not to do. His hidden, inward being, proving what his desires and dispositions are—foolish or wise, good or evil— are manifested in this will. The will is the revelation of character and life. What a person truly wills, he will infallibly seek to have done, either by himself or through others.

Your Will Be Done and Not Mine

When Jesus was suffering in the Garden of Gethsemane and said while praying, "Father, if you are willing, take this cup from me; yet not my will, but yours be done" (Luke 22:42 NIV), He was clearly stating that He had free will. Jesus chose to go to the cross and pay for our sins. Jesus suffered in the Garden to the point where He sweated drops of blood. He knew His Father's will and He chose to do it, even though it was apparently difficult to do so. And God, Who always sends us help at just the right time, sent an angel from heaven to strengthen Him while He was in the midst of His agony (see Luke 22:42–44).

This is a good example that may help us understand the price one must pay to do the will of God at times. Jesus paid a high price for our freedom, but in doing so, He opened the way for all men to be redeemed and brought into right relationship with God. The price was high, but it was worth it!

What will each one of us miss in life if we make wrong choices? I pray we never find out. How do we benefit if we live by our own self-will without considering the will of God? We may gain some momentary pleasure, but we always pay a high price once the moment passes. A man may, in a moment of passion, commit adultery, but he will pay the price in a lifetime of regret should he lose his wife, his family, and the respect of all of his friends. A young man may join a gang in order to feel that he fits in with his peers, but then spend his life in prison because of a crime committed in a moment of heated emotion. A person may spend his life not doing the things that will help him stay strong and healthy, and then regret his choices when disease leaves him weak and feeble. Let's choose to be proactive in doing what is right. Don't wait until you are forced into making a positive change by adverse circumstances.

Unless we learn the value of free will and begin to exercise it to make right choices, we will always be merely victims of life's circumstances and the bad choices those around us make. When I was a child and unable to make my own choices because I was under the authority of my parents, I was a victim of my mother and father's poor choices. But once I was away from home and had the ability to make my own choices, I was in a position to change my life. Sadly, I didn't know that, so I spent another eighteen years making wrong choices by acting according to my deceived mind and wounded emotions. At the age of thirty-six, through crying out for God's help, I received grace from Him to begin studying His Word. When I did, I discovered I could make choices according to God's will and, thus, become a victor instead of a victim.

I am letting you know you do not have to be a victim! No matter how bad your past has been, God has a good future planned for you. No matter how old you may be, it is not too late for a new beginning. You may have had a bad start in life, but you can have a great finish. All you need to do is learn the will of

> *You may have had a bad start in life, but you can have a great finish.*

God and start using your free will to choose His will. Lean on Him, depend on His grace to empower you to follow through on your choices, relax, and watch God work miracles in your life.

Another verse of Scripture in the book of John shows us clearly how man's free will, God's will, and grace work together:

> *I am able to do nothing from Myself [independently, of My own accord—but only as I am taught by God and as I get His orders]. Even as I hear, I judge [I decide as I am bidden to decide. As the voice comes to Me, so I give a decision], and My judgment is right (just, righteous), because I do not seek or consult My own will [I have no desire to do what is pleasing to Myself, My own aim, My own purpose] but only the will and pleasure of the Father Who sent me.*
>
> John 5:30 AMPC

Jesus begins by saying He is totally dependent on God, and that He can't do anything apart from Him. Jesus is referring to His humanity, not His divinity, in this verse. He listens for God's direction concerning His will and then He decides according to the will of God. *He uses His will to choose God's will!* Jesus had pre-decided that all He ever wanted was the will of God, so the daily choices that went into making that happen were a foregone conclusion and, therefore, not that difficult.

If we choose to live for God and His will, we have already made the most important decision in life—this one decision will guide all other decisions. Have you made your decision? Who and what are you living for? Have you received Christ but not yet surrendered yourself to Him? These are really important questions to ask yourself.

Make Your Own Choice

Although God does give specific instructions regarding many of our choices, there are also choices that He gives us the freedom to make. We can use wisdom, follow peace, and do what we believe God would approve of. Unless I have a specific instruction from God in His Word or by His Spirit, my general guideline is to follow what I believe to be the heart of God (His desire and will).

God will let us decide what to spend our money on, whom to choose as friends, what and when to eat, whom to marry, where we want to work, and many other things. Yet, if our underlying desire is to be in God's will, we are always listening in our hearts for anything God may not approve of—and we are ready to change if that is what God desires.

I recently had an experience that might prove to be a good example. We were going to move from our current home about one and a half miles down the road where we could build between two of our children. It sounded like so much fun and we thought it might be a good choice for the future, but I wanted to be sure. I prayed diligently and waited to get some definite guidance from God. This continued for at least six months. I knew we wouldn't be doing anything wrong if we did move, but I really wanted to make the best choice. I wanted to make the choice I would be happy with for a long, long time.

I knew it would be a lot of work and would cost money we didn't really want to spend, so I remained in indecision. I really wanted a definite yes or no from God, but He didn't give me one. It seemed clear that God was saying, *The choice is yours*, so we finally decided to keep life simple and stay in the home we have. I instantly felt relieved and knew I had made the right choice for the time being.

A great deal of the time God simply leads us by peace, wisdom, and common sense. I don't need to hear a voice to teach me not to spend more money than I earn, because that is common sense! I don't need to get a word from God about whether or not to take on more responsibility if I am already very stressed from the ones I currently have. That would not produce peace!

So my point is that we are free to make many of our decisions, but it is wise to be ready to change and follow God if His direction is different from ours. God's Word says that man's mind plans his way, but God directs his steps (see Proverbs 16:9). I highly recommend wise and thoughtful planning, but it is essential always to acknowledge God in all of our ways and give Him the opportunity to redirect us if we have chosen poorly.

We don't always make right choices, but we can always recover from wrong ones. Jesus said that David was a man after God's own heart who followed God's will (see Acts 13:22). Yet we know that David murdered Uriah, who was one of his close companions. He did this in order to cover his sin with Bathsheba, the wife of Uriah, with whom he had committed adultery, and who became pregnant as a result.

David's free will certainly caused

> We don't always make right choices, but we can always recover from wrong ones.

him to make the wrong choice in this situation, and yet God still considered him a man after His own heart, because he was repentant and truly did want to do what he needed to do in order to be forgiven and restored. We don't have to manifest perfection in order to be accepted by God, but we do need to have a heart that is committed to always finding its way back to God's will.

Chapter Summary

- God created man with free will and His desire was (and still is) that man would use that free will to choose *His* will.
- Each day can count if we learn to live it "on purpose" rather than passively drifting through the day, allowing the wind of circumstances and distractions to make our choices for us.
- We cannot always choose what our circumstances will be, but we can choose how we will respond to them. When we use our freedom to choose to do the will of God, He is honored and glorified.
- When we choose to do God's will, our intent is right, but we still need help following through and doing what we have chosen to do. It is God's grace that provides that help through the Holy Spirit.
- Regardless of your past, you can move forward, making choices according to God's will in order to become a victor instead of a victim.

CHAPTER 2

God's Will for Your Life

I delight to do Your will, O my God; yes, Your law is within my heart.

Psalm 40:8

David said that he was delighted to do God's will, and most of us would say the same thing. We are willing to do the will of God, but we may not always be sure what His will is for us. One of the questions people ask most frequently is, "What is God's will for my life?"

If we don't know the will of God, it may be that we are asking the wrong questions. We may seek answers from God about what our career should be, where we should work, whom we should marry, if we should purchase the new car we want, if we should buy or sell a house, if we should make a commitment to volunteer at church or perhaps become a missionary. Those questions are in regard to our circumstances in life and they are not wrong questions to ask, but they aren't the first or most important questions to ask. Jesus told us what to ask or seek in Matthew 6:33:

> *But seek (aim at and strive after) first of all His kingdom and His righteousness (His way of doing and being right), and then all these things taken together will be given you besides.*

Matthew 6:33

What God Desires of Us

Wanting to know God's will is not primarily about our circumstances, our job, or whom we should marry. God does care about those things, but if we seek to know those answers alone, we are not discovering the most important part of God's will.

There are deeper things that God wants us to seek Him about, and when we do we will find that the answers we need for daily life are readily evident. The following are some of the deeper things God desires that we seek Him about.

1. God desires that all men would come to saving knowledge of Jesus Christ, and through Him come to know Him personally and intimately.

When we know God deeply and intimately, we will be more likely to know the answers to questions like where we should work, whom we should marry, whether we should buy a new car, and so forth. The more intimate we are with anyone, the better we instinctively know what they would want or not want in any situation. The same things happen when we develop a more intimate relationship with God.

The apostle Paul said that his determined purpose was to know God more deeply and intimately (see Philippians 3:10). One would think that since he was inspired by the Holy Spirit to write two-thirds of the New Testament, he would have known God, and I am sure that he did, yet he wanted to know Him better and better. Is the cry of your heart to know God more deeply?

> We should not let things be more important to us than God Himself is.

I was a Christian for many years before I realized I had a very surface relationship with God. I had asked God for many *things*, but I had never asked to know Him more deeply! We should not let things be more important to us than God Himself is.

2. God desires that we become like Jesus in all of our ways, working with the Holy Spirit toward spiritual maturity and godly character (see Romans 8:29).

This is a lifelong pursuit and one that I personally find exhilarating and exciting. When we truly love God, we will want to do all that He wants us to do, and none of what He does not want us to do. We will want to be more and more like Him.

Seeking God for spiritual maturity and Christ-likeness may be the most ignored portion of God's will. Discipleship is seriously lacking among Christians, but it should be given high priority. God's will is that we glorify Him—we cannot do that if we remain spiritual infants all of our lives.

3. God desires that we know His Word because that is the only way to accurately know Him. His Word has the power to change us into His image in ever-increasing degrees of glory (see II Corinthians 3:18). It teaches us His will in every area of life.

Knowing anything always requires diligent study and a willingness to learn. It takes time and effort. Many people claim they cannot understand the Bible, but I think it is more likely that they are not willing to make the effort required to learn. The Holy Spirit will reveal the meaning of God's Word to anyone who is willing to become a serious student of it.

If we seek to know God's Word, we will find many of the answers we search for regarding daily life. One of the main ways that God guides us is through His Word. I urge you to make a commitment to study God's Word diligently.

4. It is God's will that we learn to love Him, others, and ourselves (see Matthew 22:37-39).

When asked what the most important commandment (God's will) is, Jesus replied:

> You shall love the Lord your God with all your heart and with all your soul and with all your mind (intellect). This is the great (most important, principal) and first commandment. And a second is like it: You shall love your neighbor as [you do] yourself.
>
> Matthew 22:37–39 AMPC

Since learning to love God, others, and ourselves is the most important commandment, it is a subject that we should spend a great deal of time studying. I was an unhappy Christian for many years. I spent a lot of time seeking God's help and asking Him to guide me in decisions I needed to make, but I had failed to seek His will concerning walking in love. I was a very selfish person and had not realized the importance of learning to truly love in the way that God wanted me to. I began to study love and all of its aspects, and the more I studied it and walked in it, the happier I became.

5. It is God's will that we do all that we do in faith, for without faith it is impossible to please Him (see Hebrews 11:6).

The apostle Paul instructs us to live from faith to faith (see Romans 1:17). In other words, make it your goal to remain in faith

at all times. When doubt comes knocking on your door, answer with faith.

When doubt comes knocking on your door, answer with faith.

6. It is God's will that we harbor no unforgiveness toward anyone for anything (see Ephesians 4:31–32).

Multitudes of Christians seek God daily for direction concerning their circumstances while simultaneously holding grudges
against others and refusing to forgive them. I have found that
I hear from God much more clearly if I keep my heart free of
offense. Jesus said that the pure in heart will see God (see
Matthew 5:8). They will easily discern God's will for their lives.

7. It is God's will that we give thanks in all things!

> *Thank [God] in everything [no matter what the circum-
> stances may be, be thankful and give thanks], for this is the
> will of God for you [who are] in Christ Jesus [the Revealer
> and Mediator of that will].*
>
> I Thessalonians 5:18 AMPC

8. Serve the Lord with gladness!

The last time I spent some serious time seeking God about
what His will was for me for the remainder of my life, He said,
Be happy and enjoy life! So I am going to keep doing what I do
in ministry and be sure I am happy and enjoy the journey. I am
going to continue being a wife and mom and make sure I am
enjoying the journey. Let's serve God with a smile on our faces
and let Him know that He makes us glad!

The psalmist David said that we should serve the Lord with gladness (Psalm 100:2).

If you have been seeking God for His will concerning your life, I am asking that you first consider whether you are pursuing and growing in the eight areas I mentioned. If you are not, set aside your other questions and go after what God has already said is important to Him.

Doing God's Will

Knowing God's will is one thing, but doing it is another. Knowing must always be followed by doing, otherwise the knowing is powerless. Jesus gave His disciples an example of serving by washing their feet, and then He said, "If you know these things, blessed and happy and to be envied are you if you practice them [if you act accordingly and really do them]" (John 13:17 AMPC).

If you are anything like me, you find that at times you want to do the will of God—you even intend to do it—but somehow you can't seem to follow through. The apostle Paul experienced the same dilemma and describes it accurately in Romans chapter 7:

> *For I fail to practice the good deeds I desire to do, but the evil deeds that I do not desire to do are what I am [ever] doing.*
> Romans 7:19 AMPC

He went on to say that he was unhappy and pitiable and wretched and that he needed help. Then, as if he saw the light, he exclaimed, "O thank God! [He will!] through Jesus Christ. . . ."(Romans 7:24–25 AMPC).

This leads me back to what I shared previously, which is that

God wants us to use our free will to choose His will and then rely on Him and His grace to enable us to do it!

I want to make a strong point in this area, because I think there are two mistakes we can make concerning the doing of God's will. First, we may try to do God's will using willpower alone, but then we experience frustration and disappointment because we always fail. Willpower is helpful, but it only takes us so far, and then we need supernatural power to step in. Remember, Jesus said that apart from Him we could do nothing (see John 15:5), and He meant it. Of course, there are things we can attempt through sheer determination, but those attempts are often met with stress and anxiety. By leaning entirely on Jesus, we can do what God wants us to do with His power (grace), we will give Him the credit, and we will have lots of peace and joy.

Second, it is folly to think that we can have God's will without making a choice to do so. Passive people sit idly by and hope something good will happen to them, but they do nothing to ensure that it does. They may be deceived into thinking that if a thing is God's will, then God will just make it happen without them doing anything at all. For example, it is God's will for you to have a job if you need one, but you have to go look for one. We are partners with God. We have a part and He has a part. We cannot do His part, and He will not do our part.

Our part is to be willing to do the will of God, and God's part is to reveal His will and give us the power to do it. When we pray for God to solve a problem for us, He very often gives us something to do, and we can be assured He will energize us to do anything He asks of us.

The apostle James said that if we hear the Word of God but don't do what it says, we are deceiving our own selves by reasoning that is contrary to the truth (see James 1:22). Once again, we see that knowing is useless without doing, but if we don't take the proper approach to successful "doing," we will always end in failure and frustration.

Before I learned what I am sharing, I clearly remember hearing rousing sermons in church about the need for better thoughts, more godly words, and a better attitude. I agreed and was always convicted by the Word of a need for improvement, so I promptly went home and "tried" to change. Of course, I always failed because I had left God out of the picture. I was trying to do His will by willpower alone, without asking for His help (grace).

However, I could have asked for God's grace and yet been unwilling to do anything myself and still have failed. God doesn't do everything for us, but He does work through us, and we do things while leaning entirely on Him. I am working on this book today. Yes, I am working, but not without having asked God to help me do a good job. The apostle Paul said that he worked harder than anyone, but it was actually God working in and through him that produced the good results:

> By the grace (the unmerited favor and blessing) of God I am what I am, and His grace toward me was not [found to be] for nothing (fruitless and without effect). In fact, I worked harder than all of them [the apostles] though it was not really I, but the grace (the unmerited favor and blessing) of God which was with me.
>
> I Corinthians 15:10 AMPC

We are in error if we think we can do what needs to be done on our own, and we are in error if we believe God will do everything for us. The Bible teaches us that God usually works in and through people to accomplish His will.

What Do You Want?

Man's will or "what he wants" reveals more about him than anything else. If we want money more than anything, then we are greedy. If we want promotion, popularity, and applause, then we are insecure, wanting things to make us feel good about ourselves. If we want to be delivered from our difficulties more than we want to be strong in them, then we perhaps want a life of ease with no difficulty. But, if more than anything, we want God's will, then we have a right heart and will ultimately end up in the right place with the right life. What do you want?

According to God's Word, we should want Him more than anything. If we seek Him first, then all other things will be added to our lives (see Matthew 6:33). If by examining my life I find that most of my prayers are about things that I want and circumstances in my life that I want to change, then I am probably putting my own desires first, rather than God's.

About twenty years ago, I was praying one morning for all the things I wanted and felt that I needed God to do for me when suddenly He interrupted me. Have you ever been interrupted by God while you thought you were praying to God? I was praying about what was important to me, but I was not praying in the will of God. The first thing I sensed in my heart was that I needed to compare my prayer life to that of Jesus or perhaps the apostle Paul. When I did that, I was quite ashamed of the way I had been praying because all of my prayers were for something in the physical realm (things I wanted, growth of my ministry, for people who annoyed me to change, et cetera). All of Jesus and Paul's prayers were for deeper and more important things. Jesus prayed for unity among believers. He prayed that God would keep us from evil. He prayed that we would make progress in holiness or that we would be sanctified (see John 17:15–23). He prayed for God's will to be done and not His.

> *Saying, Father, if You are willing, remove this cup from Me;*
> *yet not My will, but [always] Yours be done.*
>
> Luke 22:42 AMPC

Paul also had an amazing prayer life, and yet in all of his prayers for the believers, I never found one example of Paul praying for them to be delivered from adverse circumstances or to have more money or better living conditions. What I find are prayers for believers to know God, to know our inheritance in Him and the power that is available to us as His children, for us to be strengthened in the inner man by the Holy Spirit, to know and experience the love of God for ourselves, and to be bodies wholly filled with God (see Ephesians 3:16–19).

In his letter to the Colossians, Paul prayed that believers would be filled with the knowledge of God's will and have all spiritual wisdom. That they would walk, live, and conduct themselves in a manner fully pleasing to God, steadily grow and increase in the knowledge of God, be strengthened with the power to exercise every kind of endurance and patience (perseverance and forbearance) with joy, and always give thanks to God (see Colossians 1:9–12).

In his letter to the Philippians, Paul prayed that their love would abound more and more, that they would learn to sense and prize what was excellent and of real value. He prayed that they would be filled with the fruits of righteousness (see Philippians 1:9–11). So, as with the prayers of Jesus, we see that Paul's prayers contained spiritual depth rather than mere requests for changes in circumstances.

If you compare your prayer life to these excellent biblical examples, do you perhaps feel a need to change how you pray? If not, that is great. But if you do, there is no need to be condemned; just rejoice that God is helping you see truth that will make you free.

When I realized how anemic my prayers were, God challenged me not to ask for one "thing" other than more of Him until He released me to do so. I want to share that this season in my life that lasted six months was one of the highlights of my journey with God, and it was life-changing for me. I learned to seek God for Who He is instead of only for what He could do for me. Let me stress again that God wants to do "things" for us, and we can ask Him for what we want and need, but we should not get the cart before the horse, so to speak. Always keep first things first and the rest will fall into place much more easily.

Making every day count is dependent on having a rich and vibrant relationship with God. Our prayers are important, and they don't have to be selfish and self-centered. Let's pray and then plan for God's will to be done each and every day in our lives.

Chapter Summary

- Knowing God's will is not primarily about our circumstances—it's about getting to know Him more deeply and intimately.
- The more you study God's Word, the more answers you'll find regarding daily life.

- God wants us to use our free will to choose His will and then rely on Him and His grace to enable us to do it!
- By leaning entirely on Jesus—rather than on our own willpower—we can do what God wants us to do with His power (grace).
- Jesus said that the most important commandment is to love Him and to love others as we love ourselves.

CHAPTER 3

Living for Eternity

For God so loved the world, that he gave his only begotten Son, that whosoever believeth in him should not perish, but have eternal life.

John 3:16 (KJV)

John 3:16 could possibly be one of the most well-known Bible verses, but have we stopped to think about what eternal life is, and are we prepared for it? "Eternal" means without end, so that means we will never end; we will go on forever and ever. But where will we go when we leave this earth (something that all of us do sooner or later)? The Word of God gives us only two options: (1) to Heaven to dwell with God for all eternity, or (2) to Hell where there will be weeping and gnashing of teeth. Any logical person would want to choose Heaven, and yet many live their lives as if they don't really care.

I think it is safe to say our life *here* is to be used in large part to prepare for *there*. We can use our time wisely by putting it into the will of God. We should never behave as if time is a commodity that continues to multiply in our lives. It is, in fact, just the opposite. Every moment we use is one that we never get back again, so using it wisely is important. Many people put off being in right relationship with God until another time. Usually it is because they want to do things they know God wouldn't approve

> We can use our time wisely by putting it into the will of God.

of, so they think they will choose their own time. But what if they run out of time? It is a sobering question that can provoke us to more intercession for the lost.

How many truly live for eternity rather than for the moment? Not many, I think. We often live as if there is no tomorrow, and yet tomorrow always comes. My desire in this book is to help you learn to seize each day and use your will to choose God's will. Use the day to represent God well and to prepare to live in His presence forever.

> We often live as if there is no tomorrow, and yet tomorrow always comes.

Our entrance into Heaven is not purchased with our good works, but we do receive or forfeit rewards to be received in Heaven based on our choices and works while we are here. That's why Jesus said in Revelation 22:12 AMPC:

> Behold, I am coming soon, and I shall bring My wages and rewards with Me, to repay and render to each one just what his own actions and his own work merit.

If we take this one scripture seriously and at face value, then we would be foolish if we didn't live our lives as an investment toward eternity. One good example of doing the right thing to invest in eternity is giving financial help to other people.

None of the material things I purchase here will endure forever. I won't take any of them with me, but what I do for others will last forever. The apostle Matthew made that clear in Matthew 6:20 (AMPC):

But gather and heap up and store for yourselves treasures
in heaven, where neither moth nor rust nor worm
consume and destroy, and where thieves do not break
through and steal.

It is definitely not wrong, or even a bad choice, to have material
things. All things God has created are for our enjoyment, but we
should realize the eternal value of them and not see them as more
important than they are in light of eternity. How much would our
lives change if we made all of our decisions with a view of eternity in mind? A great deal, I would imagine.

Living with the thought of eternity in mind will help us make
better choices about what we do with our time. Everything we
do can have spiritual value if we do it all for the glory of God.
However, not everything we do can be spiritual. We must attend
to many ordinary daily tasks that can often seem quite mundane.
Use your time for whatever you need to use it for, but don't waste
it! Time is valuable, and we would be wise to treat it as if it is.

This World Is Not Our Home

I am a stranger and a temporary resident on the earth . . .
                                        Psalm 119:19 AMPC

A friend of mine used to sing in our conferences, and one of his
songs that excited the crowd more than any other was about how
this is not our home—we are just passing through. We all want
and need to know that there is something better waiting for us.
It gives us the faith to endure the difficulties we may experience
while on the earth.

In Russell Crowe's 2000 blockbuster movie, *Gladiator*, his character, General Maximus Meridius, rouses his troops by reminding them, "What we do in life echoes in eternity." This type of thinking encourages us to do the right thing while we are on earth, even if it means we must give up this life in order to do so. The soldiers were willing to die for what was right and trust that their reward would be in eternity. What we do in this life has eternal implications and significance!

> *What we do in this life has eternal implications and significance!*

It is easy to get so caught up in the realities of daily living that we forget the most important reality of all: this world is not our home. I Peter 2:11 (AMPC) states that we are "aliens and strangers and exiles [in this world]." Though we have temporary earthly citizenship, our true home is in Heaven above where Jesus has prepared a place for us (see John 14:2).

I have noticed that the early believers had a strong faith that Jesus was coming soon, and that was one of the reasons they wanted to make sure their time was used for what was truly important and had lasting value. The reminder that Jesus was coming soon also helped them make good choices regarding their behavior. For example, Paul instructed the people to live unselfishly, reminding them that the Lord was coming soon:

> *Let all men know and perceive and recognize your unselfishness (your considerateness, your forbearing spirit). The Lord is near [He is coming soon].*
>
> Philippians 4:5 (AMPC)

I think we all know that if we believed Jesus would return one week from today, we would make lots of changes in our lives.

Why not live as if He might come then, because no man knows the day or the hour? (See Matthew 24:36.)

We need not ever fear or be concerned about the Lord's return if we are prepared for it. People are very interested in when Jesus will return and what we can expect to take place as time here on earth comes to an end. Jesus talked about signs of the end of the age and His second coming, and He tells us to be ready. I am often asked what I think about end times, to which I reply, "I don't know exactly when Jesus will return, but I think we should all live as if He is coming back very soon."

Our present life is not the final chapter; it is merely the opening one. We are simply preparing for the wonderful life to come. Enjoy this life on earth, but be sure you are ready for the next one, which is eternal. Some people like to believe that they will be reincarnated and come back as something else or

> *Our present life is not the final chapter; it is merely the opening one.*

someone else for another life, and that the process continues until they are perfected. To me, this is a convenient choice of belief that allows a person not to be too concerned about how he lives now. It is also not supported in Scripture at all, but was actually refuted when Paul wrote to the Hebrews that it is appointed once for man to die and then he faces judgment (see Hebrews 9:27).

If man is a true believer in Jesus, he won't face judgment concerning his salvation, but he will face judgment regarding his works or the lack thereof (see I Corinthians 3:11–15). The works we did with pure motives will endure, and the ones we did for any other reason will be burned up. In other words, if they have eternal value, they will go with us and we will be rewarded, but if not, we lose the reward, although we still go to Heaven. Knowing these things gives me a greater desire than ever to make every day count!

I don't want to just go to Heaven; I want my full reward to be waiting for me, and since that is the case, I must be careful how I live now. I love what Paul wrote to the Ephesians when he said:

> *Look carefully then how you walk! Live purposefully and worthily and accurately, not as the unwise and witless, but as wise (sensible, intelligent people).*
>
> Ephesians 5:15 (AMPC)

Are you living carefully? Am I living carefully? It is a good question to ask ourselves and then take the time to give an honest answer. What kind of attitudes and character traits are we clinging to that God doesn't approve of? How much of our time are we wasting living selfishly instead of loving and serving others and trusting God to take care of us?

Rewards in Heaven

In his book *Making Today Count for Eternity*,[4] author Kent Crockett asks the reader to imagine a World War II soldier, wounded while selflessly rescuing his fellow servicemen. When he returned to the States, he was given the Medal of Honor for his patriotic service. What was it that motivated him to put his life in jeopardy? When his life was at stake in battle, he wasn't thinking, *I'm going to risk my life so I can receive a shiny medal*. The reward was simply the nation's way of showing appreciation for his heroic actions. He risked his life to rescue his friends and defend his country's freedom.

In much the same way, we don't serve God for a reward. We

serve Him because we love Him and we love those around us. The apostle Paul said, "It is our constant ambition to be pleasing to Him" (II Corinthians 5:9). Rewards simply show us that God is pleased with our lives and that He appreciates anyone who makes the choice to do what is right.

When talking about seizing the day and living life "on purpose," it is important to live with an eternal mind-set. If our actions, our attitudes, and our ambitions are carried out with an eternal mind-set rather than a temporal one, we are certain to accomplish bigger and better things for God and the growth of His Kingdom. When we speak of God's Kingdom growing, we are referring to souls being added to it. The salvation of the lost is the important thing on God's agenda, and we have the privilege of being his personal representatives on the earth—God making His appeal to the lost through us (see II Corinthians 5:20).

A humorous anecdote is told of a man who was being tailgated by a stressed-out woman on a busy boulevard. Suddenly, the light turned yellow just in front of him. He did the right thing, stopping at the crosswalk, even though he could have beaten the red light by accelerating through the intersection.

The tailgating woman was furious and honked her horn, screaming in frustration as she missed her chance to get through the intersection, dropping her cell phone and makeup.

As she was still in mid-rant, she heard a tap on her window and looked up into the face of a very serious police officer. The officer ordered her to exit her car with her hands up. He took her to the police station, where she was searched, fingerprinted, photographed, and placed in a holding cell. After a couple of hours, a policeman approached the cell and opened the door. She was escorted back to the booking desk, where the arresting officer was waiting with her personal effects.

He said, "I'm very sorry for this mistake. You see, I pulled up behind your car while you were blowing your horn, flipping off the guy in front of you, and cussing a blue streak at him. I noticed the 'What Would Jesus Do? bumper sticker, the 'Choose Life' license-plate holder, the 'Follow Me to Sunday School' bumper sticker, and the chrome-plated Christian fish emblem on the trunk. Naturally, I assumed you had stolen the car."

I hope this cute story helps you and me to see that although we may say that we believe in Jesus, and that we are Christians, the people around us see only our actions. Our Christian beliefs must be lived out in our daily life in front of people and at home behind closed doors in order for them to be effective in building God's Kingdom.

Though we are here only for a short time, James 4:14 (AMPC) calls our lives on earth a "wisp of vapor (a puff of smoke, a mist) that is visible for a little while and then disappears [into thin air]." Our lives on earth, although short, do have eternal significance for us and for all those we come in contact with. C. S. Lewis said, "Aim at heaven and you will get earth thrown in. Aim at earth and you get neither."

Eternity Planted in Our Hearts

I have experienced a certain level of dissatisfaction no matter what I have here on earth. I was disturbed by my seeming lack of ability ever to be one hundred percent satisfied when I was led, I believe by the Holy Spirit, to the following scripture:

> *He also has planted eternity in men's hearts and minds [a divinely implanted sense of a purpose working through the ages which nothing under the sun but God alone can satisfy].*
> Ecclesiastes 3:11 (AMPC)

This says it all! God has planted a sense of eternity and a desire to live in His presence in our hearts, and nothing but God Himself can ever satisfy that desire. Earth is not our home, and although we can and should enjoy our time here, it is not our final destination.

If we could be fully satisfied with life here on earth, we might not seek God as we should, and I believe that is why God has planted eternity in our hearts. We have a feeling that surely there is more to life than what we experience on a daily basis. People who do not have a relationship with God often ask, "Is this all there is?" Thankfully, those who do know God believe that there is more—yes, much more! We are excited about it and are happy to spend our time preparing for and waiting for it. This knowledge gives us a sense of purpose, but people who have no relationship with God through Jesus Christ often express that they feel empty, useless, and as if life has no real meaning.

God gives life meaning! He is everything that is important, and I am excited about spending my time preparing to see Him face-to-face and to live in His presence for all of eternity. The pursuit of God and His will is truly the most noble journey that any of us can undertake.

Chapter Summary

- When talking about seizing the day and living life "on purpose," it is important to live with an eternal mind-set.
- It is easy to get so caught up in the realities of daily living that we forget the most important reality of all: this world is not our home.
- Our entrance into Heaven is not purchased with our good works, but we do receive eternal rewards based on our choices while we are on earth.

- Our lives on earth, although short, do have eternal significance for us and for all those we come in contact with.
- God has placed a sense of eternity in our hearts. Life is not just about the time we have here—it is about preparation for eternity in Heaven.

CHAPTER 4

The Reward of Right Choices

I have set before you life and death, the blessings and the
curses; therefore choose life, that you and your descendants
may live.

Deuteronomy 30:19 (AMPC)

Choices are something we encounter every day. All choices lead
to a specific outcome. Each day we dictate what kind of life we
will have based on the choices that we make.

I recently heard that we face over seventy decisions each day.
Many times we let our emotions, other people, circumstances, or
the culture we live in dictate the choices we make. If that is the
case, we will not end up with the life that we would truly like to
have, so we need to learn how to make choices that will give us
the results we want. It is clear in Scripture that God desires we
have a life of fruitfulness, peace, and joy, but we won't have it
unless we make choices that are wise.

I define wisdom as doing now what we will be satisfied with
later on. Sadly, many people do what feels good, or is easy right
now, and they don't think about later on until it is here and then
they don't like their circumstances. We can invest in and guarantee a good future by making wise choices today! Rick Warren
said, "Many of our troubles occur because we base our choices on
unreliable authorities; culture ('Everyone is doing it'), tradition

('We've always done it'), reason ('It seems logical'), or emotion ('It just felt right')."[5]

> If we don't make our own decisions, then someone else or something else will decide for us.

One of the ways we use the authority God has given us is by exercising our freedom of choice in a way that will give us an end result we will be happy with. If we don't make our own decisions, then someone else or something else will decide for us.

Former president Ronald Reagan once had an aunt who took him to a cobbler for a pair of new shoes. The cobbler asked young Reagan, "Do you want square toes or round toes?" Unable to decide, Reagan didn't answer, so the cobbler gave him a few days. Several days later, the cobbler saw Reagan on the street and asked him again what kind of toes he wanted on his shoes. Reagan still couldn't decide, so the shoemaker replied, "Well, come by in a couple of days. Your shoes will be ready."

When the future president did so, he found one square-toed and one round-toed shoe! "This will teach you to never let other people make decisions for you," the cobbler said to his indecisive customer. "I learned right then and there," Reagan said later, "if you don't make your own decisions, someone else will."[6]

What Are You Doing with Your Time?

All of our choices are important, and they have either a positive or a negative impact on our life, but in this book I want to deal mainly with the decisions we make regarding the use of our time. How much of it do we waste, and how much of it do we spend wisely? Are we putting our time into what will help us be the person we truly want to be, or will we end up someday disappointed and bitter because "life" didn't turn out the way we hoped it would? "Life" doesn't just turn out to be one way or another without any input from us. Although we certainly cannot control all of our circumstances and the things that happen to us, we can control a lot of them by making a commitment to know God's will for us and then make decisions accordingly.

The world is filled with people who are resentful and angry because their life isn't what they want it to be, but if we could closely examine the choices they have made during the course of their lives, we would usually find that their poor choices are behind their dissatisfaction. The problem is that unless they realize that, take responsibility for it, and make positive changes, they are stuck in a situation that will not ever change.

Nick Vujicic was born with no arms or legs and he said this: "Often people ask how I manage to be happy despite having no arms and no legs. The quick answer is that I have a choice. I can be angry about not having limbs, or I can be thankful that I have a purpose. I chose gratitude."[7]

Nick's choices had nothing to do with his lack of limbs, but they had everything to do with how his life turned out. We all have things in our lives that we don't like and would not have chosen if we'd had a choice, but we can all choose how we react to them. My brother and I both grew up in very adverse circumstances and I am living a fruitful, wonderful life, but he died in an abandoned building at the age of fifty-nine. The difference in our lives is the result of the attitudes we decided to have about the past and the choices we made about what to do with the time we had left in life.

I wasted several years of my life being angry, resentful, discouraged, and depressed, but, thankfully, I finally decided to do something good with the time I had left. If you want to start today using the time you have left on this earth, then it begins with a decision to seize the day every day and be an individual who lives life "on purpose" for a purpose. Every moment of our lives does not have to be regimented and fit into a plan, but, on the other hand, if a good portion of our time isn't put into something with purpose and meaning, it will be wasted.

We must get rid of the idea that everything that happens to us is based on some huge cosmic plan that we have no authority over. God has given us free will, and His wisdom is available to help us make choices that will produce a life we can be proud of and enjoy. In Psalm 119:109 David said, "My life is continually in my hand, yet I do not forget Your law." David was basically saying, "I can do what I want to, but I choose to live according to Your Word." Every "I will" or "I do" that we see in Scripture is a declaration of man's right to choose.

One Day at a Time

God gives us grace to live one day at a time. He tells us not to worry about tomorrow and to trust Him for each day as it comes. Although we are to live life one day at a time, it is still prudent to have a plan for the future. If we have goals we want to reach, it will help us to organize each day in a way that will enable us to reach those goals.

Let's make each day count for something. How do I want to feel by the time I go to bed tonight? I want to be satisfied that I made the best choices I could, and that I put my time into what I truly wanted to put it into. Last night, I was not satisfied when I went to bed because I had spent too much of the evening trying to watch television, and I kept having to turn the programs off because they were either plain ridiculous or I was not comfortable with their content and language. Even though I wasn't satisfied with my choices from yesterday, I can make better ones today.

Getting each day started right is important. We are more likely to be satisfied with the outcome of any day if we get it started right. The first thing I always choose to do is start my day with God. You can spend a long time or only a short period of time with Him, but the only way to get your day started right is to start with God. Talk to Him, ask for His help and guidance in all you do, and submit your day to Him for His direction. Take in God's Word in some form through studying, reading, listening, or watching. Whether it is one verse of Scripture or an entire chapter in the Bible, it will help you.

> The only way to get your day started right is to start with God.

David was committed to seeking God in the morning. He said:

> In the morning You hear my voice, O Lord; in the morning
> I prepare [a prayer, a sacrifice] for You and watch and wait
> [for You to speak to my heart].
>
> Psalm 5:3 (AMPC)

When we go to God first, before other things, it is a way of honoring Him and saying with our actions, "Apart from You, I can do nothing" (see John 15:5). You might even consider lying in bed for five minutes after you wake up and use this time to talk to God about your day. This is especially a good idea if you have small children or an extremely busy household that is active from the moment you get out of bed.

David said that he would watch and wait for God to speak to his heart (see Psalm 5:3). What can we expect when doing this? I started my day with God, and, of course, I asked for His help in writing today. I didn't hear any specific instruction, but I believe He is giving me ideas as I think about the manuscript. If we submit our day to the Lord, instead of just planning it on our own, He can work through our thoughts, causing them to be in agreement with His will. We may think we have a great idea, but it is actually because God has placed the idea in us.

> Roll your works upon the Lord [commit and trust them wholly to Him; He will cause your thoughts to become agreeable to His will, and] so shall your plans be established and succeed.
>
> Proverbs 16:3 (AMPC)

After having begun your day with God, now take some time to think about your day and what you would like to accomplish. You and I can both approach each day with purpose. Let me give you an example of how I planned my day today:

I woke up and talked with God awhile. I got up, made my coffee, and spent time with God in prayer, and I read part of a book about prayer. I made a plan to write until noon, then go to the gym and work out and take a walk. Next, I will shower, wash my hair, and get dressed. I will probably have a cup of coffee and a snack. I will then either write some more or take care of phone calls I need to return. I will meet Dave for dinner and enjoy time with him and my food. We will come home and spend the rest of the evening resting and will probably watch a movie.

I have arranged this day so I can get some work done, exercise, walk outside, take time for proper grooming, have time for enjoyment, and get good rest. I will also fellowship with God throughout the day, giving thanks for His presence and asking for help in the things I do. Planning your day and managing your time doesn't mean that you have to work all the time, but you do need to do what you do on purpose! Even if I decide to lie on the couch all day and watch movies, I should do it because I planned to do it, and not because I was cleaning house and saw the couch, lay down, and turned on the television and stayed there all day while thinking, *I should not be doing this.*

The fact that I planned my day doesn't mean everything will go exactly the way I planned, but at least I have a direction and a purpose in mind. People full of purpose make the most of the time and talents God has given them.

Each day is different and presents different responsibilities and challenges, so we get to plan each one accordingly. Some days I may work all day, other days I may be with family and friends all day. Planning variety in our schedules is very important if we don't want to get bored with life.

I am training myself to go through this thinking process every day because I want to channel my time into things that will bear good fruit. I refuse to waste my life. I only have one and don't get another when this one is gone, so I want it to count.

I have looked at the week, the month, and the year, and I have a vague idea of what I need to do and accomplish, where I need to be, and what I have to do to get there. I have long-range and short-range goals, and I am hopeful that you do also, but we still have to take life one day at a time if we want to enjoy it and not feel overwhelmed. What we choose today is part of what we want to happen even in the distant future.

You may have heard the statement: "Men plan and God laughs." It is a cute statement and has value, but I also think that perhaps when man has no plan he has no direction. Have a plan and work your plan, but always be open to letting God change your plan just in case you have the wrong one.

When Things Don't Go According to Plan

No matter how well we plan, things rarely go exactly according to our plan. Some of the interruptions we deal with could be avoided if we stood more firmly on our decisions, but many of them can't be. Any tendency you might have to feel guilty or condemned when you don't meet your goals is not only useless, it is actually counterproductive. If I don't accomplish what I want to today, I simply reroute it for tomorrow. But at the same time, I also am watching my life and trying to learn from experience how I can stay more on track. I want to allow interruptions that cannot be avoided, but I don't want to allow unnecessary things to get me off course. I cannot expect other people to keep me on track because that is something I have to do. I should not blame the people who interrupt me if I am not willing to take the responsibility for allowing their interruption. I may not be able to keep someone from calling me at the wrong time, but I don't have to answer the phone! Or I may have to answer a call, but I don't have to get into a long conversation about something that isn't necessary.

Some people are more naturally gifted at staying focused than others are, but anyone can improve through practice. I am usually a fairly focused person, but I know several people who struggle with staying focused. Sticking to a plan is more difficult for them, but it is not impossible. "Do the best you can and keep growing" is always my advice. Our

> Do the best you can and keep growing!

relationship with God is not based on our plan for the day, or how organized we are, and He loves us unconditionally. However, living life "on purpose" is the only way we are going to end up being the person we truly want to be and enjoying the best life we possibly can.

Part of the problem we all face in our society today is that most of us are simply trying to do too many things, and "too much" of anything, even a good thing, usually becomes a bad thing. We should only do what we can do peacefully, and when peace leaves, we need to reroute and do whatever is necessary to get it back.

We make our schedules, and only we can change them, so instead of running frantically through life trying to do it all so we please everybody, we can learn to say no at the proper time. If I ask a crowd how many of them feel they have too much to do, almost everyone raises their hand. God never intended His people to live under excessive stress and pressure. Life is to be thoroughly enjoyed, and that isn't possible if we constantly feel pressured by an excessive schedule that causes us to rush frantically through the day.

Part of becoming an "on-purpose" person is developing an ability to schedule your life in such a way that you are well balanced in all areas. That is why when I plan my day, I almost always schedule time for relaxation and enjoyment as well as work.

You will enjoy your life much more if you take proper time for you! You are not being selfish if you take care of yourself, because the best gift you can give your family and friends is a healthy you.

Chapter Summary

- Each day we dictate what kind of life we will have based on the choices that we make.
- Wisdom is doing now what we will be satisfied with later on.
- The best choice you can make each day is to begin that day spending time with God.
- You can approach each day with purpose. Make a plan and stick with it.

CHAPTER 5

Where Did All the Time Go?

Lord, remind me how brief my time on earth will be.
Remind me that my days are numbered—how fleeting my
life is.

Psalm 39:4 (NLT)

At the end of every year, we probably say and quite often hear, "I can't believe this year is already over," or "I can't believe it is Christmas again already." We regularly hear things like, "Time flies by," "Where did all the time go?" and "My children are grown and I barely remember them growing up." You will find it interesting if you begin to really listen to all the comments that we make about time. Most of us indicate by our words that we don't have enough of it and that it goes by faster than we can comprehend.

However, time moves at the same speed now as it always has, so how fast it goes by must have something to do with the choices we make. We all have the exact same amount of time each day. We have the same number of hours, minutes, and seconds, yet some of us are very frugal with them and accomplish great things, and others—far too many others—are wasting time. They use it for wrong purposes or they make the mistake of thinking there will always be plenty more of it. No one of us knows exactly when our time on earth will be up. Each day that God gives us is a present, and that is why it's called the "present." We want to unwrap the gift carefully, cherish it, use it fully and wisely, investing it in something that we will be proud of later in life.

If you are old enough to remember them, you can sit around and talk about the good ole days when life was slower all you want to, but it won't bring those times back. What we must do now is manage our time so we get the most benefit from it we can. This Scripture pretty much says it all, and it is one of my favorites:

> Look carefully then how you walk! Live purposefully and worthily and accurately, not as the unwise and witless, but as wise (sensible, intelligent people).
>
> Making the very most of the time [buying up each opportunity], because the days are evil.
>
> Therefore do not be vague and thoughtless and foolish, but understanding and firmly grasping what the will of the Lord is.
>
> Ephesians 5:15–17 (AMPC)

In those three verses of Scripture, God tells us:

1. To be careful about our time and choices.
2. To be an "on-purpose" person.
3. To live a life worth living.
4. To really think about what we are choosing to do and make wise decisions
5. To make the most of our time.
6. Not to let opportunities pass us by.
7. Not to be passive, vague, thoughtless, and foolish.
8. To know the will of God and grasp it firmly.

I want to urge you to ask yourself questions as you read this book. I doubt it will do you much lasting good if you just read it for something to do, or merely to read my latest book. Ask yourself things like: "Am I making the most of my time?" "Am I firmly holding on to God's will for my life and refusing to let anything steal it?" "Am I living life 'on purpose,' or letting circumstances and people control my destiny?" "Am I satisfied with my choices, at least most of the time?" "How often do I say, 'I don't know where time goes'?" "Am I seizing each day God gives me, and making the most of it?"

I have come to the conclusion that I have a responsibility to know where my time goes and to slow down long enough to inventory what I am doing with it, and to make sure it is what I really want to do. One thing I enjoy doing is looking at my calendar, where most of the things I do are written down, and reviewing it. It provides two things for me: (1) the opportunity to remember what I have done and perhaps enjoy it all over again, or (2) at the very least, to learn from any mistakes I may have made by spending time doing things that I now wish I had not done. Another thing I do regularly is lie in bed at night and go over my day, remembering what I did from the time I got up that morning.

Sometimes I find that I did more than I thought I did. At other times, I realize that although I had a plan, God interrupted it and guided me in a direction He wanted me to go in. And reviewing my day also gives me an opportunity to determine if I used the day wisely or wasted it. Did I let myself get sidetracked by something unimportant? Did I lose my focus on what was really important and end up doing none of what I truly wanted to do? Perhaps I got online to look up something and somehow ended up watching cute YouTube videos for three hours. I did that this morning, but, thankfully, it was for only about thirty minutes, and Dave asked me if I was watching cartoons! There is certainly nothing wrong with watching cute YouTube videos unless it is merely distracting you from something else you really need to accomplish.

I doubt that any day goes by that I stay on track all day and don't waste any time. We are humans with inherent weaknesses, but we can improve and grow if we pray and confront areas in our lives that are out of order.

Don't Waste Today Worrying about Yesterday

One thing you don't want to do is get up in the morning and realize you pretty much wasted yesterday, and then waste today feeling guilty about your poor choices yesterday. Zig Ziglar said, "Worrying does not take away tomorrow's troubles, it takes away today's peace."

One day this week I had my prayer time in the morning, as I always do, and I fully intended to stay in close fellowship with God all day; however, when evening came I realized I had stepped out of my office after prayer and hadn't even thought about the Lord the rest of the day because I was busy, busy, busy! I started feeling guilty, or perhaps just disappointed in myself, when the Lord reminded me not to waste today regretting yesterday. His mercy is new every morning, and we can always begin again!

The next evening I was amazed at how often the Lord was in my thoughts and what great fellowship we had all day, but I strongly believe that I would have missed that opportunity if I had continued in my regrets. I was reminded that God is with me even when I am not consciously aware of Him, and that He understands that I am growing, and He sees my heart! The same is true for you.

Most days, my goals are greater than my ability to accomplish them, and that doesn't bother me if I have at least made some progress toward fulfilling them. No matter what we get done, there is always something left to do, so I highly recommend that you celebrate what you did accomplish and get up the next day and begin again. Perhaps a good goal to begin with if you need help in this area is to choose at least one thing you want to accomplish each day instead of burdening yourself with unrealistic expectations and feeling like a failure.

> *Choose at least one thing you want to accomplish each day.*

When you do fail or make mistakes, the best thing to do is to admit them and let them be a tutor for your future. Our mistakes can be valuable if we learn from them.

Spending Time

One day I was taking a shower and talking to the Lord, more or less just verbalizing my feelings, and I said, "Lord, I feel like I spend a lot of time just taking care of myself." I was thinking of how the dentist wants me to brush my teeth three minutes each time I brush, and always floss, and, because I have lots of crowns on my teeth, he wants me to get them cleaned every three or four months. I have doctor visits and checkups, I work to take care of my skin, I get my hair cut every two weeks, I work out with a trainer three times a week, and, if at all possible, I walk four to five miles each day. And of course I must get my fingernails done! I take nutritional supplements and make an effort to eat good, healthy food and drink lots of water.

I am constantly packing and unpacking clothes I have carefully picked out so I can look my best at my conferences. Sometimes I get weary of doing these things over and over, and then I remember that I won't like my harvest if I don't sow good seed. Anything you would like to have, you will need to ask God to give it to you and then be ready to do whatever He leads you to do. You sow the seed and He brings the harvest! Most people want to be healthy, strong, and look their best, but not everyone invests in helping to make that happen.

I was pondering these issues and others about time, and it came to me strongly that all of us have the same amount of time, and we do *spend* it. I spend time in these areas I have mentioned as well as in many other areas. Time cannot be stored up and used later. Each day we spend our time, and once it is spent we cannot get it back. If we purchase something with money and we aren't happy with it, we can usually take it back to where we purchased it and get our money back or exchange it for something else, but time is not like that. Once it is gone, it cannot ever be regained, and that is why we seriously need to use our time wisely! We want to invest our time, not waste it.

> Each day we spend our time, and once it is spent we cannot get it back.

It is wise to spend time resting, worshipping and praying, studying God's Word, relaxing, laughing, developing personal relationships, and enjoying life, as well as accomplishing the fulfillment of career and financial goals. I also believe it is wise to invest time in ourselves. When I said to the Lord, "I feel like I spend a lot of time taking care of myself," I didn't feel at all that He chastised me. I didn't feel selfish or self-centered, because I know if I don't take care of myself, I won't be around for the completion of my journey with God. I fully intend to finish what God has called me to do. I feel that I am investing part of today in my God-ordained future, and it is not a waste.

May I respectfully say that you might greatly benefit if you spent more time taking care of "you." You would last longer, feel better, spend less time at the doctor and less money on medicine. You could spend the time being healthier or you will spend the time taking care of physical problems, but either way, you will spend the time.

I just had a complete hip replacement, and the doctor said the surgery was a breeze because I was in good shape and had great bone density. I healed very quickly, so I saved lots of time because I had invested time exercising previously! On the other hand, I have only six teeth that don't have crowns on them because I didn't take time to go to the dentist very often when I was younger. I didn't get my teeth cleaned regularly, and I didn't floss. I did brush my teeth, but obviously not well enough. I was "busy" and didn't want to use my time for that, so I ended up spending a great deal of time and money to repair the result of my poor choice!

Are you spending your time on things of value that benefit you now and later on? If not, you can make a change. Consider these three things:

1. Your life is yours and you can take charge of it.
2. Your time is yours and you can put it into God's will for your life.
3. Your schedule is yours; if you don't like it, remember that you made it, and only you can change it.

> Your time is yours and you can put it into God's will for your life.

These are things that God has taught me over the years, and I hope that sharing them with you will help you use your time more wisely.

Making changes in your life often takes time. If a huge ship were going in the wrong direction, it would take some strategy and time to turn it completely around. It is the same way with a life that is going in the wrong direction. Don't be impatient, but be committed to finding out and firmly grasping the Lord's will for your life.

What to Choose When You Can't Do It All

When we fail to use our time wisely, it is always due to poor choices, but it is possible that our heart is entirely right and that we are simply trying to do all we think is expected of us. Most of the years when I did "too much" and traveled "too much" and tried to please other people "too much," I didn't realize I was doing anything other than trying to do what was right. It took several years, and a few bouts with stress-related sickness, for me to realize that if I were doing what was truly right, then I would be getting better results.

God has not called us to be sick, worn out, and miserable. As a matter of fact, He promises just the opposite.

> Come to Me, all you who labor and are heavy-laden and overburdened, and I will cause you to rest. [I will ease and relieve and refresh your souls.]
>   Take My yoke upon you and learn of Me, for I am gentle (meek) and humble (lowly) in heart, and you will find rest (relief and ease and refreshment and recreation and blessed quiet) for your souls.
>
> Matthew 11:28–29 (AMPC)

If we are following Jesus and His way of doing things, we will be energetic instead of tired and worn out. We will live in peace, and we will experience contentment. He leads us beside the still and restful water, and it is there where He restores our souls (see Psalm 23).

Jesus and the disciples were ministering to people in great need. There were so many people coming to them that they had no time to eat or rest. So what did Jesus do? He said, "Let's go off by ourselves to a quiet place and rest awhile" (Mark 6:31 NLT). Amazing! Jesus walked away temporarily from valid needs in order to take care of Himself so He could finish what God had sent Him to do.

When you can't do it all, you should choose the best thing for the present time. Jesus knew that it was better to let the needs of the people wait momentarily so He and His disciples could rest and eat. This allowed Jesus to be properly prepared to meet their needs in due time.

Today, I ended up with too many plans and too little time, so I had to make some choices. I chose not to go for my walk and used the time writing this book. I knew that if I didn't make any progress on the manuscript, I would not be happy with myself. I will walk tomorrow, but for today, starting the book was more important. I have reached the end of too many days and not been happy with my choices during the day, and that is something I want to avoid in the future.

When you can't do it all, remember there is a time for all things—everything is beautiful in its time (see Ecclesiastes 3). Being in God's timing is equivalent to being in His will. If you are doing something in God's timing, it will be beautiful and fulfilling in every way.

Chapter Summary

- Time is a gift to unwrap carefully; cherish it, use it fully and wisely, and invest it in something that you will be proud of later in life.
- We have a responsibility to know where our time goes and to slow down long enough to inventory what we are doing with it.
- Regardless of how much you get done, there is always something left to do, so celebrate what you did accomplish and get up the next day and begin again.
- Time cannot be stored up and used again later. Make the most of the time God has given you today.

CHAPTER 6

Ways to Avoid Wasting Your Time

Making the very most of the time [buying up each opportunity], because the days are evil.

Ephesians 5:16

I doubt that you want to waste your time (I know I don't want to waste mine) and yet we all do to some degree. So let's take a look at some of the ways it happens:

1. When you complain a lot about your busy schedule, that is a good sign that you need to make some changes in it.
2. We cannot do everything and do anything well.
3. What do you let hijack your time?
4. Are you just busy, or are you productive?
5. Are you able to stay focused on what you really want to do?
6. Do you spend more time talking about the things you need to get done than you actually spend doing them?
7. Do you buy time by getting less sleep and then lose time because you are tired?
8. How often do you make mistakes because you were in a hurry?

9. How often do you have to repair something because you didn't want to spend the money to do it right to begin with?

10. Do you deal with little problems in order to prevent them from becoming big problems?

In order to make the most of the time God has given us, let's look at some of these things a little more closely.

Complaining

Complaining is a negative practice. It is almost always done by those who either have circumstances they don't want and cannot do anything about, or those who don't like their circumstances and simply *won't* do anything about them, but either way, complaining is useless and changes nothing. Prayer combined with taking action according to God's guidance is the only answer to any problem we have. God's Word teaches us not to worry and to cast our care, but it never says we are to cast our responsibility.

> *Complaining is useless and changes nothing.*

Quite often the people who complain the loudest are the ones who do absolutely nothing to help change the circumstance they are complaining about.

Don't waste your time by allowing unnecessary interruptions, or by not disciplining yourself to stay focused and then complaining about how little time you have. When we complain we remain in the same situation, but if we are willing to take responsibility and make positive changes, God will give us direction as to what to do.

Taking positive action to change something we don't like is

much easier on us than passively complaining about it. God created us to be active, and we simply don't function well unless we have the mind-set to find solutions to our problems instead of murmuring and being unhappy. God will definitely show us what to do if we are willing to do it!

While we are waiting for our breakthrough, God's Word instructs us to give thanks in all things! Replace all grumbling with gratitude and you will find solutions to your problems quickly.

> *Give thanks in all circumstances; for this is the will of God in Christ Jesus for you.*
>
> I Thessalonians 5:18 (ESV)

Priorities

A priority is something that is regarded as more important than another thing. When we say, "I don't have time," what we are really saying is, "It's not my priority." Hopefully, most of us believe that what we do is important or we would not spend time doing it, but certain things must always be more important than others. We have to have the ability to know which things in our lives are the most important to us and then be sure that we make time for them. If we don't, we will spend our lives doing what is urgent rather than what is important. We usually do what we truly want to do, but rarely do we admit it. If we are not doing what we know in our heart we should be doing, we often excuse our behavior by saying that we didn't have time. I have only heard one person say, "I don't exercise because I don't want to," but I have heard

Our time belongs to us, and we can prioritize it wisely if we truly want to.

hundreds say that they don't have time. Our time belongs to us, and we can prioritize it wisely if we truly want to.

The apostle Paul prayed for the believers that they would learn to sense what was vital and approve what was excellent and of real value (see Philippians 1:9–10). Even though what we are doing might be good, it may not be the best thing.

People frequently ask me how I manage to keep my priorities straight since I have a lot going on in my life, and I always reply that I am constantly straightening them out. I find that I have to examine my life regularly to make sure I am not letting it get out of balance. My relationship with God is the most important to me, so that must come first in my time and attention. My family is next, so I always make time for them. I just told someone this morning that no matter what I am doing, I always take calls from my children if at all possible because I never want them to think that the ministry is more important to me than they are. My health is also important, and I put time into maintaining it. Obviously, the ministry God has made me a steward over is very important and that requires a great deal of my time.

I must admit that I was often out of balance in several areas of my life in the earlier years of my ministry. I was very busy and had not learned some of the things I know now, and I sometimes let things that were less important take precedence over things that should have been more important. Thankfully, God covers some of our mistakes when we lack knowledge, but when we do have knowledge, He expects us to make right choices.

Don't Major in Minors

You may have heard the statement "Don't major in minors," or "Don't strain at a gnat and swallow a camel." They both refer to not giving importance to matters that in the long run are not really very important.

I have heard my friend John Maxwell teach that we should put 80 percent of our time into the top 20 percent of our strengths. Most people waste their time trying to strengthen weaknesses that may only improve very little no matter how much effort they put into them, while ignoring the development of their strengths and truly excelling at them.

If everything is a priority to us, then nothing is a priority, and we live confused and frustrated lives. Some people try to do everything, so they do nothing really well. Are you able to focus on what is truly important and always make sure you give those things the attention they deserve? If not, that is a good place to begin becoming an "on-purpose" person who is able to seize the day! At our ministry we often say, "Be sure the benefit we reap from a project equals the time put into it."

> *Some people try to do everything, so they do nothing really well.*

Time Hijackers

We all have things that waste our time, but we may or may not be aware of what they are. If someone had a history of hijacking airplanes, he or she would definitely be on a "no fly" list, and our time hijackers that we are aware of should be on a "no admittance" list. In other words, they may knock on the door of our time but we won't let them in. If you are not aware of what hijacks your time, simply take one week and watch your life and you will get an education.

The modern communication technology like cell phones, e-mail, Facebook, Twitter, Facetime, and instant messaging (to name a few) can be time hijackers. If we have them, we can't blame them for beeping at us, because they are simply doing what they were made to do. It is our responsibility to ignore them unless we truly want to find out what message they are giving us. Although these modern conveniences have a benefit, we don't have to let them control us.

At the very least, we need to learn to see who is trying to contact us and, if we are busy with a higher priority, ask ourselves if it can possibly wait. Every time we are interrupted, it takes time and effort to get back to what we were doing, and sometimes we never get back to it. These modern conveniences may be some of the biggest culprits of the growing lack of ability of people to focus on what they are doing.

People can also become hijackers of your time. Some people will keep talking even after you tell them you are not able to talk right now! They think their emergency trumps anything you may have planned. If you know which individuals are likely to talk either too long or about something that is a waste of time, it is best not to answer, or perhaps text and tell them you are unable to talk at the time.

It is often the unexpected that steals our time. We run into a friend unexpectedly and he or she would be offended if we didn't take time to talk, so we lose thirty minutes we planned to give to something else. We have a repair we didn't expect and that takes time; the Internet is out and we were depending on it for a project; the dog gets sick and has to go to the vet. Things like this cannot be avoided—they are merely part of life—but if there is anything we can control, it is our responsibility to do so. Just in order to not be frustrated, I usually allow time for interruptions in my scheduling because I almost always have some, and then if I don't get interrupted I feel like I received a gift of time I wasn't expecting.

Often we are our own worst enemy when it comes to wasting time. I might be focusing on preparing a message for one of my seminars and I look out the window for a moment and notice the mailman delivering my mail. I immediately go to get it and spend the next hour and a half opening it and then disputing a bill I had already paid. Did I have to get the mail at that moment? "No" is the honest answer. I went to get it because I was curious, and it would have been better had I waited until I was finished with my message.

To be a person who lives life "on purpose," we will have to be relentless in dealing with things that get us off the track we want to be on. The more we do it, the easier it will become, but let me be clear that living the life you truly want to live will be something you will have to be firm about. Not everyone may understand your determination, but you will be the one who will accomplish great things instead of living with regrets over what you wish you had done with your life.

Methods of Buying Time

Do you buy time by getting less sleep and then waste time being tired and feeling bad the next day? This is a temptation for a lot of people. I've been told that half of Americans get less sleep than is recommended, and that is seven to eight hours each night. There are a few people who don't need much sleep, but very few. Most of us need good-quality sleep in order to be energetic and pleasant rather than cranky. We need rest to be able to be creative and able to focus. If my mind is tired from lack of sleep, it is more difficult for me to keep it focused on what I am trying to accomplish.

I have come to a point in my life where I realize one of my

greatest needs is energy! When I am tired or don't feel well, it affects every area of my life adversely. I no longer buy time by giving up sleep or rushing continually, because I have learned the hard way that I always lose time in the end. It may be visits to the doctor, or making unnecessary mistakes because I am tired, but it will always cost me eventually.

Do you try to buy time by rushing through projects? If we don't do a thing right the first time, we will probably get a chance to do it over. When things are not done right, they steal time later. It may be our time or someone else's, but it will happen. We have recently dealt with a chimney and roof problem that required lots of time with a repairman and was expensive. The entire reason for it was that the job wasn't done properly to begin with.

Doing a thing right or in an excellent manner always takes more time than merely doing it quickly just to get it done and check it off of our list. Some personality types just want every project off their list, and they often make mistakes in judgment because they don't wait for wisdom. I make quick decisions and sometimes I cost myself time because I didn't think a thing all the way through.

Be Frugal but Not Foolish

I used to waste time and gas running around looking for a sale for everything I needed to buy. I was adamant that if I couldn't get it on sale, then I wasn't going to get it, but my attitude was wrong. It developed from years of having barely enough money to get by on, but God showed me I was often spending more money trying to save money than I would have spent had I purchased what I needed and gone home.

I have experienced driving across town to get a pair of shoes that were advertised on sale and finding they were out of them and were not getting any more in stock. They had the same shoes in my area, but they cost five dollars more, and I wanted to save money so I spent four dollars in gas money and lost two hours. It is interesting to me to look back and see how my out-of-balance attitude cost me! Some people take pride in seeing how little they can spend on an item. They feel like they are beating the system, but are they really?

Let's imagine that we are building a house and we are offered two insulation packages for the walls. One is good, but not as good as the other one. The better one will cost two thousand dollars more, but we don't want to spend the money so we decide to go with the less expensive kind. After moving into the house, we feel that our heating and cooling bills are quite high for the size of the home. After having an expensive expert come in, he informs us that the insulation in our home is not very good, and because of that our bills will always be higher. We only have two options at this point: We can try to add insulation to the home, but that will be very costly since the home is already built, or we can pay the high cost of utility bills.

When making a purchase, it may be worth it to drive across town if we are going to save a significant amount of money, but at least call to see if the item is in stock before making the trip. It may not be worth it to spend more on insulation, but we should consider all the options and not make a decision based solely on cost unless we have no other option.

I am prudent, but I really try not to be foolish. My time is valuable; as they often say, "Time is money." If you have not realized yet that your time is valuable, I suggest you think it over, because time may be one of the most valuable things you have.

Dealing with Small Things

The Bible states that the little foxes spoil the vine (see Song of Solomon 2:15). That means that little things unattended to may turn into things that cause big problems. Let's say a couple is buying a house and they have found one they really like, but on a walk-through the man noticed in the corner of a closet what looked like it might be mold. He knew his wife would be disappointed if he found any reason for them not to accept the house. He was a person who had a tendency to notice what was wrong with things and this irritated his wife, so he thought, *I don't want to cause trouble and it probably isn't mold anyway.*

They bought the cute house, and after living in it a while everyone in the family started getting sick. After a great deal of time and money spent on doctor visits, it was discovered that there was indeed mold in the house. It was hidden in the walls where it could not be seen. Although the problem was eventually dealt with, it cost a lot of money to get rid of the mold because it had been spreading, and the home had to be torn apart, which created quite a mess and lots of frustration.

If the man had tended to the small thing he saw in the corner of the closet, just think what it would have saved him.

I actually know a family this happened to, and I can assure you that the man wished with all his heart that he had taken the action and the time to have the "little thing" checked out before purchasing the home.

We often compromise in order to get what we want when we want it, or in order not to have to spend time on something we don't want to spend it on, but compromise always costs us in the long run.

> Compromise always costs us in the long run.

Sometimes we don't do a thing just because we don't want to and for no other reason. It is of course our privilege to choose, but then we should not complain if what we didn't do turns into something more for us to do eventually.

These few things I have mentioned can be time wasters, and there are thousands of others. It is wise to find the ways we waste time and ruthlessly eliminate them from our lives. Do today what you will be happy with tomorrow, and then tomorrow you won't regret what you didn't do today!

> Do today what you will be happy with tomorrow, and then tomorrow you won't regret what you didn't do today!

Chapter Summary

- Setting priorities helps you deal with the urgent but focus on the important.
- Prayer—not complaining—is the best step to take when facing a problem.
- Time is one of the most valuable things you have.
- In order to seize the day, it is important to stay on task in your life. Don't let unnecessary interruptions steal your time.
- Take time to pray and ask God, "Is this the best way I could be spending time right now?"

CHAPTER 7

We Only Get One Life

I will not waste my life! I will finish my course and finish it well. I will display the gospel of the grace of God in all that I do. I will run my race to the end!

Apostle Paul (Acts 20:24; paraphrased
by John Piper, *Don't Waste Your Life*)

It is good to remember that we only have one life to live, and then we will come face-to-face with God, who will ask us to give an account for ourselves. That is why Paul said in Romans 14:12, "And so each of us shall give an account of himself [give an answer in reference to judgment] to God."

This is not intended to frighten us, but to urge us to realize that eventually the time we have been given will run out, and we will be asked to give an account of what we have done with it. This scripture doesn't frighten me, but it does urge me to be sober-minded about my life and use it to please God.

It is sobering to think that every hour that ticks by is one that we will never get back, so we should make it count. Don't waste it! I have wasted a great deal of time in my life, and you may feel the same way. What have we spent time on that, when we look back, we realize

> The wise man always lets
> his mistakes educate him.

has produced nothing good? The wise man always lets his mistakes educate him.

In the last chapter, I talked about specific ways we might avoid wasting time, but there are others, and they are ones that are more hidden. They are hidden because they are issues of the heart. They are tormenting emotions that we permit to remain in our lives, sometimes for years, and each day that we do not confront them is another day we have wasted.

If any one of us intends to seize the day, enter into intentional living, and stop wasting time, we cannot successfully do so unless we face the truth about how much time we waste on things like guilt, fear, worry, anxiety, jealousy, envy, greed, resentment, hatred, bitterness and unforgiveness, self-pity, et cetera. If we want to seize the day, we must be prepared to seize negative emotions that will rob us of the day. Emotions that we don't want may visit us quite suddenly, without an invitation from us. All it takes is for someone to swoop in front of us and grab the parking place we have been waiting for at the mall, and we get a visit from anger. Or for someone we work with to get the promotion that we believe we deserve more than they do, and we get a visit from jealousy, resentment, and anger.

Because we never know on any given day what our circumstances may be, and because we cannot control the actions of other people, we are in danger every day of wasting time on negative, useless emotions. It is quite possible that there are more people in the world right now who are either experiencing some of these emotions or are angry about one thing or another than there are those who are totally at peace.

Jesus said that the makers and maintainers of peace would be called the sons of God (see Matthew 5:9), and understandably so. Sons have a degree of maturity. We don't expect anything other than unbridled emotions from babies and children, but we do expect more than that from our grown sons and daughters, and so does God.

For too long, we have allowed ourselves to be victims of these energy-draining, time-wasting emotions, thinking we can't help the way we feel, but the truth is that we can control our emotions and not allow them to control us. It may not be easy, especially if you are someone who has lived by emotions for a long time, but it is possible with God's help.

> *He who has no rule over his own spirit is like a city that is broken down and without walls.*
>
> Proverbs 25:28 (AMPC)

God would not instruct us to rule over our own spirit if it were not possible to do so. We need not be victims of circumstances, for through God's grace (power), we are created to rule, to subdue, to manage, and to have authority.

I have found it very helpful to resist negative, unwanted emotions at their onset. When something happens that causes unwanted emotions to rise up within you, subdue them. If you let the emotion lead, you are headed for trouble. Name the emotion and say, "You're not welcome," and then start talking to yourself. For example: If I were to hear of a ministry opportunity a friend had received and it was one I had always dreamed of, I might get a visit from jealousy and envy. As soon as I notice it, I should say, "Jealousy and envy, you are not welcome here!" Then I can have a talk with myself, saying, *Joyce, you are so blessed that it would be ridiculous for you to be jealous of anyone. God has a unique plan for each of us and, Joyce, you have done things that others have never done, and some of them will do things you will never do*. I always find when I do this that my emotions calm down and I can behave properly.

Yes, I have had to have conversations like this with myself often in my life, and others that are similar. I have told myself often that I don't intend to waste my day being angry or feeling sorry for myself. Perhaps this type of action is a new thought for you, but the truth is that we all talk to ourselves, if not out loud at least in our thoughts, so why not tell yourself something that will help you live the life you truly want to live.

When a person is threatening to jump off of a building, someone is sent to "talk him off the ledge." I use this idea when I feel like I am about to leap into a state of wild emotion. Sometimes we have only a few seconds to decide what we will do, but if we can learn to take a deep breath and talk to ourselves, we may save ourselves a lot of trouble.

Let's imagine that my husband, Dave, says something I don't agree with and refuses even to admit that he might possibly be wrong. Most married women know what I am talking about! When this happens, I can feel anger rising up within me, and I need to do something about it before it reaches my mouth. I know this because of many years of navigating this scene improperly and then regretting it later.

I have *wasted* a great deal of time being angry with Dave over things that were so insignificant and foolish that it was ridiculous. But once we get angry and start talking, or perhaps yelling, it is hard to be talked off the ledge because we have already jumped, so to speak. But if I can talk to myself and remind myself quickly that my goal in life should not be to correct Dave and prove myself to be right, I will save myself a lot of misery. Only those who intend to seize the day will rule their emotions.

I guess we will never know for sure, but I seriously wonder how many days of our lives we have wasted, never to be redeemed, due to harboring these negative emotions. It is probably best that we don't know, or else we might lose another day in regret.

I think I will talk about some of these emotions in groups because we often find that they work together in attacking the purposes of God for our lives. Jesus said that the new commandment He gave us was that we love one another as He had loved us, so that the world might know we are His disciples (see John 13:34–35). Since God is love, the only way the world can see Him in action is through love, and God has called us to let Him love the world through us. Therefore, let's look at emotions that hinder the love of God from flowing through us and make us miserable in the process.

> Since God is love, the only way the world can see Him in action is through love, and God has called us to let Him love the world through us.

Jealousy, Envy, Greed, and Resentment

All of these emotions are condemned by God and should be aggressively avoided by us. Each of them is a total waste of time because they don't change our circumstances. They don't help us get what we want. They do make us mean-spirited and grumpy.

Always wanting more no matter how much we have shows a greedy spirit. We are told to avoid not only greed, but also greedy people, so it must be a dangerous thing indeed. God wants us to be content with what we have, ask Him for what we want and need, and trust that He will provide it in the right way, at the right time, if it is the right thing for us.

These evil emotions certainly present themselves to all of us, and merely feeling them is not sin, but when we nurture these emotions with evil thoughts we usually act on them and they become sin. Always pray for God to help you resist the devil the moment any negative emotion shows up in your life.

Are you jealous of anyone? Do you have resentment in your heart because you feel left out? Take a step of faith and tell the person you resent that you are happy for him. Taking godly action always breaks the power of the devil. We overcome evil with good (see Romans 12:21). Go a step further and start praying for the person, asking God to bless him even more. The more you bless others, the more you will be blessed.

Don't waste any part of the one life you have to live being jealous, envious, greedy, or filled with resentment!

Worry, Anxiety, and Fear

These three emotions are ones I think it is safe to say everyone experiences at different times in their lives, but like the first group we examined, they are a waste of time because they accomplish nothing positive. They don't prevent or solve our problems. They help nothing, and they harm us, because they steal our peace and joy. Henry Ford said, "I believe God is managing affairs and that He doesn't need any advice from me. With God in charge, I believe everything will work out for the best in the end. So what is there to worry about?"[8]

Only a deep trust in God can help us avoid these useless emotions. Our trust in God increases as we have experience with Him and see His faithfulness in our lives. God is good, and He always takes care of us. He may not do exactly as we would have preferred, and we may not always understand why, but He is good and He is faithful.

Why do we worry? It may be a difficult thing to face, but I

think we worry simply because we are afraid that we won't get what we want. If we can say, "Your will be done, Lord, and not mine," and mean it, we will never have to worry again. All fear is a result of not fully understanding the unconditional love of God and then not trusting that, because He loves us, He will always do what is best for us. "Perfect love casts out fear" (I John 4:18 NKJV).

I once read that a day of worry is more exhausting than a week of work. This is another good reason not to worry. Most of us don't have any excess energy to waste, so the next time you are tempted to worry, just remember that if you do, it will be

> A day of worry is more exhausting than a week of work.

a waste of time. Corrie ten Boom said, "Worry doesn't empty tomorrow of its sorrow, but it empties today of its strength."[9]

Anger, Unforgiveness, Hatred, and Being Offended

Jesus said many times that we are to forgive those who hurt us and do so quickly. He doesn't make light of our pain, but He does know we only add to it through these miserable emotions. The emotions of anger, unforgiveness, hatred and bitterness, and offense are close relatives. When we become angry, we may refuse to forgive and we get bitter and can even begin to hate those God has called us to love.

Let us be more concerned about our reaction to those who hurt us than we are about what they have done to us. What they have done is ultimately between them and God, and our reaction is between God and us. We will need to be prepared to forgive many people in our lives, and some of them over and over again. Being angry with people is useless. It very rarely, if ever, changes them, but it does harm us in many ways. Forgiveness is an attribute of

> Forgiveness is an attribute of strong people.

strong people. The weak find it hard to do. I've heard it said that one of the keys to happiness is a bad memory. Let's remember the good that people do and forget the bad.

Don't be easily offended unless you are signing up to be miserable in life. We have countless opportunities to be offended each week, but we don't have to "take offense" just because it is offered to us. Sane, reasoning people don't do things that will make them miserable.

Guilt

I probably wasted more time feeling guilty than anything else. Until I was in my fifties, I suffered from what I can honestly say was continual guilt. I even felt guilty about feeling guilty because I knew it wasn't what God wanted for me. I often say, "I didn't feel right if I didn't feel wrong!"

My guilt started at the time I was a small girl due to my father sexually abusing me and warning me not to tell anyone. I assumed it had to be wrong if I couldn't tell anyone, and this started a cycle of guilt in my life that was unbelievably tormenting. When a person feels guilty she can't really enjoy anything.

God wants us to enjoy our lives, but we can't do that if we don't

> God has provided total forgiveness and guilt-free living in Jesus.

know how to enjoy *ourselves*, and we can't do that if we continually find fault with ourselves. God has provided total forgiveness and guilt-free living in Jesus (see Isaiah 53:5–6). Our debts have been paid. Our sin and the guilt have been removed, so any guilt we suffer with is the devil's way of deceiving us and preventing us from receiving the fullness of God's love.

The way God helped me experience freedom from the torment of guilt was to be well educated on what His Word says about it, then to believe His Word more than I believed how I felt. I would often say out loud, or quietly to myself, *Joyce, this guilt you feel is a liar and a thief. You are forgiven completely, and your sin is removed as far as the east is from the west. If there is no sin, how can there be any guilt?* I actually learned to reason with myself based on Scripture, and although it took some years to be completely free, I made progress on a regular basis.

Self-Pity

Self-pity is surely a waste of time because it does not move God to give us what we want. We feel sorry for ourselves when we don't get our way, or feel slighted in some way. People do sometimes take advantage of us and that of course is not right, but self-pity won't change it. This is another negative emotion I wasted a lot of time on until God spoke this to my heart: *Joyce, you can be pitiful or powerful, but you can't be both, so make a choice.*

I will leave you with this thought as we move on to other things: Your time is valuable, so don't waste any of it on negative, useless emotions that do nothing but make you miserable.

Chapter Summary

- Your life doesn't have to be run by your emotions. You can make the decision to control your emotions instead of them controlling you.

- In order to enjoy your life, it is important to learn to be content. God wants us to be content with what we have, ask Him for what we want and need, and trust that He will provide it at the right time.
- Worry, anxiety, and fear harm us because they steal our peace and joy.
- Only a deep trust in God will help us avoid useless, time-wasting emotions.
- God has provided total forgiveness and guilt-free living in Jesus.

CHAPTER 8

Determination

I am too positive to be doubtful,
Too optimistic to be fearful,
And too determined to be defeated.

Unknown

Determination is a quality that will make you continue trying to do or achieve something that is difficult, or the act of officially deciding to do something. Leonardo da Vinci said, "It had long since come to my attention that people of accomplishment rarely sat back and let things happen to them. They went out and happened to things."[10] Determined people are rare, but nothing in the world can take the place of determination and persistence. Talent doesn't take its place, education doesn't take its place, and neither does any level of genius. The world is filled with common men and women who have done uncommon things, and all of them had determination. I am of the opinion that nothing good happens accidently.

Determination triumphs over any deficit we can name. Anyone who wants to have determination can have it. It doesn't belong to a privileged few. You might say, "Well, I am just not aggressive," but making progress in life does not require a naturally aggressive personality. It simply requires that you be determined to make your life count.

Life is challenging, unpredictable, and busy. Life throws us curve balls, and we swing hoping to make contact. So how do we live an "on-purpose" life in a world full of distractions? The answer is one word: determination! Determination keeps us going when the going gets tough. It helps us keep our eyes on the prize, not being easily distracted by the things that are painful and frustrating. It helps us practice good habits until they become a natural part of us.

> *Determination keeps us going when the going gets tough.*

As believers in God and His good plan for our lives, our determination is driven by something far greater than our own sheer will. We must have the help of the Holy Spirit, and that help is always available to those who will ask and believe. This is our greatest source of strength and power, and it enables us to overcome the obstacles in our path and achieve a life of purpose. If you have very little determination and tend to give up easily, then at least begin making a change by praying that God will work determination in you. Believe that He has heard and answered you, and then step out in faith, trusting that the feelings you desire will come as you go forward. The excuse that we don't feel like doing a thing that is right is a pitiful excuse. I doubt seriously that Jesus "felt" like going to the cross and dying for the sins of mankind, but He did it, relying on something much deeper than His feelings. He relied on the power of God to enable Him, and looked forward to the joy that was on the other side of the pain.

What Do You Believe?

It is often a mystery to me why some people are so determined and others are not, but I think I have found one reason, at least. Some people don't believe in themselves! They have a bargain-basement view of who they are and what they can be with God on their side. If you are a Christian and you have very little or no confidence, it is because you have failed to realize what God has done in you through a new birth in Christ. When we receive Jesus as our Savior, we are born again, and we receive a new nature. The nature we receive is that of God! He places His qualities in us as seeds that carry unbelievable promise of harvest in our lives if we will water them with His Word and nurture them by working with the Holy Spirit to keep the weeds of worldliness from choking them.

Any born-again person is a new creature, and nothing from the past has any power over him unless he allows it to.

> *Therefore if any person is [ingrafted] in Christ (the Messiah) he is a new creation (a new creature altogether); the old [previous moral and spiritual condition] has passed away. Behold, the fresh and new has come!*
>
> II Corinthians 5:17 (AMPC)

Our new life with God cannot truly begin until we understand this Scripture verse. Without it, we will always see ourselves the way we were. We have a book of remembrance of all our failures recorded in our memory, and detailed records of everything anyone has ever told us we could not do. The simplicity of it is that we don't see what God sees. He believes in us, but we don't always believe in us. We either don't know, or we don't believe that God lives in us through the Holy Spirit, and we don't see what we are capable of through Him.

I was a churchgoing Christian for many years before I knew this truth. I had a sad past, and was on my way to a future with even more sorrow, but I began to study God's Word seriously and made the decision to take the promises I found and apply them to my life. Once I believed them for myself, I was unstoppable! My journey has been long, and at times very difficult, but when we have faith, it motivates us to keep going. Faith sees in the Spirit what the eye cannot see in the natural. Faith does not rely on feeling or emotion, but it relies on God, Who is faithful and true.

> *God is faithful (reliable, trustworthy, and therefore ever true to His promise, and He can be depended on); by Him you were called into companionship and participation with His Son, Jesus Christ our Lord.*
>
> I Corinthians 1:9 (AMPC)

You can believe that "you can," or you can believe that "you can't," and either way you will be right. No matter how many wonderful things God wants for us, or our family and friends want for us, unless we want them and are determined to have them, they will pass us by. We will drift through life very often being jealous of people who have what we want but being unwilling to do what they did to get it.

> *You can believe that "you can," or you can believe that "you can't," and either way you will be right.*

God's plan for everyone is not the same, but His plan for all of us is good! We can't all do the same thing, but we can all do something amazing. We can live the best life we can possibly live. Believe it and receive it! That is a spiritual law of the Kingdom of God. We believe His promises, we ask for them, being ready to wait for His timing in faith, and we will receive them. We receive them by faith, and we will see them manifest in our life at the proper time.

*Whatever you ask for in prayer, believe (trust and be confi-
dent) that it is granted to you, and you will [get it].*

Mark 11.24 (AMPC)

It is very difficult for us to believe what we cannot see or feel,
but faith is the assurance of what we cannot see. We take the
promises of God as fact, and we decide to live according to them.
I cannot see gravity, but I believe in it because I am not floating
in the air right now. Sitting in my home today, looking out my
window, I cannot see the wind, but I am aware that it is blowing
because I see the trees moving. We cannot see God, but we can
see the things He does in our lives, and even if those things are
small, they encourage us to believe for better things. Do you see
the things that God has done in your life, or do you stay busy
seeing what He has not done yet? If you do that, you will become
quickly discouraged and give up. Take time every day to thank
God for every tiny thing He has provided for you, and as you do
it will increase your faith. Even in the midst of great difficulty, we
can continue thanking God, believing that He can and will work
good out of it.

Handfuls on Purpose

There is a woman in the Bible named Ruth. She was at one time
an idol worshipper, but she decided to make a change and believe
in the one true God. Ruth had desperate circumstances, but
God had a good plan for her. There was a man named Boaz who
was a very wealthy man with a great deal of farming land. His
field-workers were reaping in the fields, and Ruth had come to
glean in those same fields. She was there to pick up the leftovers
that the reapers missed, but Boaz noticed her. Have you ever felt

like all you have had in life were the hand-me-downs and the leftovers? Even so, if you put your faith in God, He will do something amazing in your life. If you feel like Ruth, God can cause a Boaz to notice you, too. In other words, God can give you favor and lift you up out of the ash pit of life. He gives us beauty for ashes (see Isaiah 61:3) and lifts us out of the pit we find ourselves in (see Psalm 40:2).

God put it in Boaz's heart to tell the reapers to leave handfuls of grain for Ruth on purpose. What she found in the fields was perhaps not a lot, but it was enough for the time being. Eventually, she married Boaz and things changed dramatically in her life. God will also leave "handfuls on purpose" for you, but you cannot complain about them as if they are of no account. Perhaps you don't have as much as someone else you know, or as much as you want, but you can be thankful and excited about what you do have.

Further study of Ruth's life shows great determination as she made the choice to remain with her widowed mother-in-law instead of returning to her homeland, where she would have had plenty. She chose the more difficult path because she believed it was the right thing to do. Initially it seemed to cost her, but eventually it brought a harvest into her life. (For the whole story read the book of Ruth in the Bible.)

If we don't disrespect the handfuls God leaves us on purpose, we will someday be the one leaving handfuls for others. God will bless you and make you a blessing!

When Do We Need Determination?

We always need some degree of determination. It takes some determination just to get out of bed in the morning, but there are times when we need more determination than other times. What are those times?

When the Way Is Hard

When our way in life is hard, it requires more determination to keep going than when the way is easy. It is easy to begin a thing, but God is looking for finishers! Anyone who intends to have anything good, to be good, or to do any good will be attacked by the devil. We often say that if the devil isn't bother-

> If the devil isn't bothering you, then perhaps you are not bothering him.

ing you, then perhaps you are not bothering him. According to Scripture, he roams about like a lion roaring in fierce hunger, seeking whom he may seize and devour.

> Withstand him; be firm in faith [against his onset—rooted, established, strong, immovable, and determined].
>
> I Peter 5:9 (AMPC)

We may encounter hard things, but we never encounter things that are impossible with God. He promises not to allow more to come to us than what we can bear. He knows each of us intimately, and one of the ways He makes us strong is by permitting us to go through difficulty. The only way a bodybuilder can build more muscle is by lifting heavier weight. God allows us to be in places and situations that require us to stretch our faith.

When you are facing a difficulty, don't say, "This is too hard; I just cannot take it." Instead, agree with God's Word and say, "Through Christ, I can do this. I am determined to do the will of God and go all the way through every difficulty and into the best life God has for me." Trust me when I say that the words you speak are important to your future success. God calls those things that do not exist yet as if they already do. (See Romans 4:17.)

To trust God only when things are easy is not the way to spiritual growth. Growth requires challenge. Even as children grow from their teen years into being young adults, they face what to them seem like insurmountable challenges. A friend of mine has a grandson who has just started college, and he has a girlfriend he adores. He also has a variety of things he loves to do that would come under the heading of "entertainment." He is finding it difficult to work part time and do all of these other things, and is having difficulty understanding why he has to give up some of the things he "likes" to do in order to do what he "needs" to do. His parents see very plainly what he needs to do, but this is a new road for him to walk, and it is challenging. It sounds simple to us, but to him it is hard! Little does he realize that these types of choices will continue throughout his life, and they will prepare him for new levels of promotion.

His parents are tired of arguing with him, so they told him that he didn't have to work, but they would not be giving him any money. They are, of course, not trying to be unkind to him, but they have to teach him that he cannot merely do what he feels like doing throughout his life and still have the kind of life he wants to have.

This sounds like a simple thing that everyone should realize, but the world is filled with millions of adults who still have not faced this truth. God works with us at all times trying to help us mature, and the sooner we cooperate the faster we will get good results.

Here is the bottom line: We will go through hard things, and when we do, we can determine not to give up, but to press through. We can do so with a thankful heart and a good attitude, trusting God every step of the way.

When God Moves Slowly

God rarely moves according to our timetable, but what we count as slowness is not that way to God (see II Peter 3:9). He is much more interested in excellence than speed. He is turning us into individuals who can represent Him in an excellent manner. He wants vessels that are always available to Him and ready to do as He asks at all times. This being the case, we absolutely cannot be in a hurry. A masterpiece is never created in a hurry.

> *A masterpiece is never created in a hurry.*

Learning patience is one of the prerequisites for spiritual maturity. When we accept an inferior product rather than waiting for an excellent one, we always make a mistake. Slow down, enjoy the journey, and don't rush. Life is short, and rushing only makes it shorter!

Focusing on what we want is the thing that makes waiting so difficult. We can choose instead to focus on God and use the extra time we have while waiting to grow in Him. God is good, and He will not withhold anything good from us unless it is for a good reason. I spent years frustrated because my ministry grew so pitifully slowly, and at times I even felt that it went backward for a season. I could not understand why God wasn't doing what I was asking Him to do. No matter what I did, God didn't move any faster.

Of course, now I look back and understand all too well that I wanted something that I was not spiritually mature enough to have, and God in His mercy withheld it. The attitude I had while waiting was in itself proof that I wasn't ready for more. Why should God ever give us "more" of anything if we are not thankful for the things He has already given us, no matter how small they are? Always remember that a delay is not a denial, and when God seems slow, be determined to stand firm.

When the Way Is Lonely

I have often found that following God can be lonely. The people we depend on the most for support and encouragement can disappoint us. They often misunderstand us, and may even criticize us for the path we have chosen. Even in this, God has purpose. It is important that we look to God and not to people. We all love approval, but we must not need it in order to obey God. If we do, we will surely be defeated.

Jesus must have been lonely at times. There even came a point when He was suffering on the cross that, in his humanity, He felt forsaken by His Father. Yet, even that didn't cause Him to give up. He had already made the quality decision that He would do God's will no matter what it cost Him.

The pain we endure at various seasons in life is temporary, and it is very important to remember that when we are going through it. "This too shall pass," is one of my favorite sayings. The sun always shines after the storm!

No matter what might be causing us to want to give up, we can be determined to press on. If we give up, it will only mean we have to start again at another time. We'll still need to face what we ran from the first time!

Chapter Summary

- Nothing in the world can take the place of determination and persistence.
- Determination helps you practice good habits until they become a natural part of your life.
- Confidence and determination come by knowing who you are in Christ Jesus and the promise of new life God has given you.
- Faith is the assurance of what we can't see. It fuels our determination to stand on God's promises and accomplish His plan for our lives.
- You may encounter difficulties, but choose not to give up. Nothing is impossible with God.

CHAPTER 9

Seize the Day

Yesterday is gone. Tomorrow has not yet come. We have only today. Let us begin.

Mother Teresa

From what I have learned over the years, this is a summary of what the word *seize* means: to take hold of forcibly and suddenly, or to grab, grasp, or snatch. It also means to take control of or to repossess. When we seize something we subdue it, and that is exactly what God told Adam to do concerning the earth.

> *And God blessed them and said to them, Be fruitful, multiply, and fill the earth and subdue it.*
>
> Genesis 1:28 (AMPC)

If we desire to know how God wanted man to live, we can look to the beginning of time as we know it, and there is no better place to look than Genesis chapter 1. God created Adam and Eve and gave them authority and dominion over the rest of His creation. He told them to subdue it, or, in other words, to seize it and use it in the service of God and man.

Far too many people are inactive, and they wait for something to fall into their laps—they end up waiting until it is too late. They live unsatisfied and unproductive lives simply because they

don't wake up each day ready to seize the day and make the most
out of it.

We can easily see God's will for man, but sadly, Adam and Eve
chose their own will instead of using their free will and power of
choice to choose God's will. They did what God told them not to
do. They sinned and God's plan for man was damaged, but not
entirely lost. The devil deceived them into thinking that having
their own selfish desire would make them happy, and for a short
while he thought he had ruined God's plan for man. However,
God had an amazing and powerful plan for the redemption of
man. A plan that, if followed, would allow him to take back all
that the devil had stolen.

The devil is referred to as "the thief" in the book of John. He
comes to steal, kill, and destroy, but Jesus came to redeem and
restore (see John 10:10). What has the devil stolen from you? Perhaps you have never even thought about it. Has he stolen your
confidence, your courage, your identity, your energy, zeal, and
enthusiasm for life? Has he taken your peace and joy? What
about your right standing with God as His child? Do you know
who you are in Christ and the privileges your inheritance from
Him gives you?

The devil stole my childhood through sexual, emotional, and
mental abuse. Fear took the first thirty-two years of my life, but
Jesus has given them back to me in double measure. God promises not only restoration, but He promises to give us back double
what the enemy has stolen (see Zechariah 9:12, Isaiah 61:7). In
one scripture He even promises a seven-fold return on what a
thief has taken (see Proverbs 6:31)!

When we lack correct knowledge, the devil takes advantage
of us, but once we know the truth of God's Word it makes us
free. The term *makes us free* doesn't mean that freedom magically

happens with no action on our part. The truth we apply to our lives is what will make us free. Just the realization that we don't have to live as victims, but that we actually can wake up and seize the day is in itself freedom!

A Victim Mentality

A victim is someone who is harmed by another. A victim is involved in an unfortunate situation—the victim of a car accident, a fire, a robbery, or someone who has been abused. The victim is harmed and was unable to do anything to prevent the harm. Many people are victims of various unfortunate situations, but they can recover with God's help unless they develop a "victim mentality" and refuse to let it go.

I was a victim of sexual abuse, and for many years I lived as a victim. I felt sorry for myself, used my past as an excuse for a bad attitude and bad behavior, and had a chip on my shoulder, a feeling that the world owed me preferential treatment because I was a victim. That wrong attitude never made my life any better, it just kept me trapped in the pain of my past.

God's Word tells us to let go of the past and trust God to be our vindicator. It is, of course, not easy, but it is easier than remaining a victim. God wants to give us victory, but we need a victorious mind-set. Where the mind goes the man follows (see Proverbs 23:7). If our thinking is according to the truth found in God's Word, then our living will ultimately be what God intended for us also.

If you have been a victim and you feel that the things you suffered are still affecting you, try this: Lie in bed for a few minutes after waking up and think some thoughts on purpose. Think like this: *This is the day God has made and given to me as a gift. I will not* waste it! *My past is behind me, and nothing from the past can have any effect on me if I don't allow it to. God is on my side, and I choose to live this day energetically, enthusiastically, and passionately. By the grace of God, I will get up and put my time into things that have purpose. I resist the devil, and he will not steal my time today!*

Be prepared to do this day after day, and you will soon begin to see results. It takes time to renew the mind, so don't be disappointed if you do not get immediate results. It is great if you do get them, but at least be prepared not to give up and to be determined to keep doing the right thing. Beginning each day with this mind-set helps you get your day started right.

Perhaps millions of people lie in bed each day and think, *I don't want to get up. My life is miserable. Nothing good ever happens to me. All my life people have taken advantage of me. I hate my life and I dread facing another day.* I woke up daily for many years with some version of this type of thinking. I was miserable, and I made myself more miserable with my own thoughts and attitude. I was unaware that I could do anything about my life, so I remained a victim. But, thank God, He has given me the victory through Christ! He wants to give that same victory to anyone who has been a victim and needs redemption.

> *But thanks be to God, Who gives us the victory [making us conquerors] through our Lord Jesus Christ.*
>
> I Corinthians 15:57 (AMPC)

Living Life on Purpose

Seizing the day means that we live life "on purpose." We don't wait for things to happen to us; we happen to things! We live aggressively, we take action, we think, we plan, and we go for the best! We are born with a temperament chosen by God, and admittedly we are not all alike. Some people are naturally more driven than others, but God has not ordained that anyone be passive, inactive, apathetic, and purposeless. No matter

> We don't wait for things to happen to us; we happen to things!

how God has designed you, it is important that you become fully you and that you glorify God with your life.

When I suggest that we live life "on purpose," that doesn't mean we all have a world-shaking purpose. Our purposes vary at different seasons of our life. When I was eighteen, my purpose was to get away from my father who was abusing me, get a job, and become able to take care of myself. By the time I was twenty-three, I was divorced, a single parent, and lonely. My purpose was to survive, pay my bills, find good child care, and, hopefully, someday be truly loved. When I was thirty, my purpose was to raise the three children I had by then, learn to be a good wife, keep my house clean, cook three meals a day, and live within a very limited budget.

God was part of my life from the age of nine, but a very small part. I kept Him on the sidelines of my life for emergencies only. Although I was a Christian, I had no idea what was available to me as a believer in Jesus. I continued to struggle through each day with a sour attitude, doing the best I could to live life.

By the time I was forty, I had embarked on a much more serious relationship with God. I was studying His Word and actually working at a church and teaching a Bible study. I was in the process of healing from all the emotional wounds I had and was beginning to see that I no longer had to be a victim. Now I am over seventy and have lived life "on purpose" for many, many years. I know the results firsthand of living as a victim and living with victory. Victory is available to everyone, but it must be seized. It will not merely happen to us. It is a gift from God and is given by His grace, but the devil is always lurking close by, hoping to steal what God offers. We must therefore live with intention, purpose, and an attitude that says, *I will have what belongs to me as a child of God! I will not be cheated! I will seize the day!*

The apostle Paul had this attitude, and we can see it clearly in his letter to the Philippians. He wrote that he intended to take hold of that for which Christ Jesus had taken hold of him:

> *I press on to lay hold of (grasp) and make my own, that for which Christ Jesus (the Messiah) has laid hold of me and made me His own.*
>
> Philippians 3:12

In the same chapter of the Bible, Paul also made a firm statement declaring his determined purpose. He said that his determined purpose was to know God and the power of His resurrection that lifted him out from among the dead even while he was in his body (see Philippians 3:10–11). Wow! I can feel the power of Paul's determination. He knew what God wanted for him, and he was going to seize it, subdue it, and take back all the devil had stolen from him through deception.

Just writing these things increases my passion to live life to the fullest, and I hope reading them does the same thing for you.

Seize the Kingdom of God

The devil is actively at work, and he is relentless in his pursuit of doing evil. This Scripture describes him well:

*He lurks in secret places like a lion in his thicket; he lies in
wait that he may seize the poor (the helpless and the unfortunate); he seizes the poor when he draws him into his net.*

Psalm 10:9 (AMPC)

The poor spoken of in this verse refers not only to those who
have a financial lack, but also to those who are poor in being
loved, knowing truth, or having spiritual knowledge. The poor
are those who are downtrodden and disadvantaged in any way.
Satan waits to take advantage of us, but God is ready to rescue
and redeem. The choice is ours. Whom will we believe? Will we
sink into our pain and wallow there, or rise with determination
in our hearts and seize the life God sent Jesus to purchase for us?

God's Word makes it plain that we will need to *seize* the Kingdom because we have an enemy who is working to steal it from us:

*And from the days of John the Baptist until the present time,
the kingdom of heaven has endured violent assault, and violent men seize it by force [as a precious prize——a share in
the heavenly kingdom is sought with most ardent zeal and
intense exertion].*

Matthew 11:12 (AMPC)

A closer look at this scripture in the original language it was
written in reveals that Jesus is stating that the Kingdom of God
has suffered attack, but the "energetic" take it by force. The Kingdom of God has suffered violence, meaning it has suffered attack.
Satan is relentless in attacking God's Kingdom and His purpose
in the earth. However, there is an answer to the situation. The
violent (the energetic) take it by force. They take back what the
devil has stolen. They are determined, and they seize each day for

the purposes of God. I like the language of the Amplified Bible in this verse: "A share in the heavenly kingdom is sought with most ardent zeal and intense exertion."

If you feel that you are lacking this kind of drive and energy, I recommend that you begin praying for it. I pray the following prayer often: "I ask for energy, zeal, enthusiasm, and passion to live this day. Let me be an on-purpose person who seizes the day and uses it in the best way possible."

I am not a lazy person, but neither am I a high-energy, bounce-out-of-bed-each-day-with-exuberant-zeal type. However, I am very determined, and that overrides any lack of feeling I might have. Recently it occurred to me that I might pray for those feelings. After all, the Bible says we have not because we ask not (see James 4:2). After I prayed, as so often is the case, God led me to do some specific things like eating more protein and taking some additional nutrition that was not part of my regimen. As I have mentioned, God answers prayer, and one of the ways He does this is by showing us what we need to do. You won't get a good result if you pray for energy, then you don't get enough sleep, eat junk food, are nutritionally depleted, get no exercise, and have a negative mind-set. With God, all things are possible, but they are not automatic. We must cooperate with Him and take obedient action. When Jesus' mother asked for a miracle from Him, she then turned to the people and said:

> *Whatever He says to you, do it.*
>
> John 2:5 (AMPC)

They did as He commanded, and they got their miracle. It is often just that simple! There are situations where no matter what we do, nothing changes and we need to wait patiently for God to do what no man can do; however, if He asks us to do something, we certainly need to do it.

As I have continued to pray and do the things God is leading me to do, I have had a noticeable increase in actual physical energy, and it feels good! Energy makes every day better, so I encourage you to think about this area of your life, pray, and then do your part in taking good care of yourself so you can become the healthiest person you can possibly be.

The apostle Mark gives us another thing to ponder in his letter:

> But no one can go into a strong man's house and ransack his household goods right and left and seize them as plunder unless he first binds the strong man; then indeed he may [thoroughly] plunder his house.
>
> Mark 3:27 (AMPC)

Earlier in Mark chapter 3, a crowd had gathered against Jesus and was accusing Him of doing the works He did with the help of Beelzebub (the devil). They said He was casting out demons with the help of the prince of demons (see Mark 3:21–26).

Jesus answered by telling them a parable. He said that no one could enter a strong man's house and rob him unless he first bound the strong man. His meaning was that He was setting people free and doing the miracles He did because He was first binding the strong man (the devil) who was causing their problems. The lesson for us is that we also can bind the devil and keep him from stealing our lives, but it requires action.

Sometimes the simple choice to be active keeps the enemy bound. He works through passivity, laziness, and inactivity, but when we are actively doing what God has given us to do, the enemy finds no open door into our lives.

What should you do if you know what you should do but you just don't want to do it enough to make you take action? I think this is a valid question and one that we should deal with. I can write one hundred books on what to do, but people won't do it unless they possess a "want to" in their spirit that overrides any resistance in the flesh.

I recommend that you focus on Jesus, how much He loves you and what He has done for you. As you receive His love and let it amaze you, you will find yourself wanting to do all that He asks you to do. The development of your personal relationship with God is very important, because it is the foundation for all obedience. Jesus said, "If you [really] love Me, you will keep and obey My commandments" (John 14:15). The apostle John wrote that we love Him because He first loved us (see I John 4:19); therefore, receiving God's love will cause you to love Him in return, and out of that love you will obey Him.

> What should you do if you know what you should do but you just don't want to do it?

Struggling to do the right thing by willpower alone only helps to a small degree. When we run out of our own strength, which we all do, then we need the power of God (His grace) to bring us through to the finish. Because this book is filled with encouragement for you to be aggressive, active, enthusiastic, passionate, and filled with zeal, it is also important that I warn you of the dangers of "works of the flesh." These are things we try to do in our own effort and strength that can only be done with God's help. "God, help me" is one of the most important prayers we need to pray throughout each day of our lives.

The things I am encouraging you to do in this book are not things you need to do in order to be saved or to be loved by God. Those are free gifts! I simply want you to live the best life that

God has for you by encouraging you to seize each day and use your time wisely.

We need mega doses of God's grace in order to do what is right, and His grace is always available and it abounds and overflows. He offers us grace and more grace! All the help we need is available if we will ask and receive. Jesus said to ask and keep on asking (see Matthew 7:7). If you feel weak in determination, passion, zeal, or enthusiasm, don't think this book is just not for you. It is especially for you, because God has a purpose and a plan and you are a big part of it. Keep reading, keep praying, and believe that today is your day for something great. Remember:

Yesterday is gone. Tomorrow has not yet come. We have only today. Let us begin.

Mother Teresa[11]

Chapter Summary

- The truth of God's Word sets you free.
- Victory comes when you have a victorious mind-set, not a victim mentality.
- Seizing the day means we live life "on purpose."
- You can choose an attitude that says, "I will have what belongs to me as a child of God! I will not be cheated! I will seize the day!"
- When we are actively doing what God has given us to do, the enemy finds no open door into our lives.

CHAPTER 10

Scheduling and Planning

*Cause me to hear Your loving-kindness in the morning, for
on You do I lean and in You do I trust. Cause me to know
the way wherein I should walk, for I lift up my inner self
to You.*

Psalm 143:8 (AMPC)

As the Scripture verse above suggests, it is wise to begin each
morning asking God to show us the way He wants us to walk and
requesting His help in following through. Pray and then plan! If
we will acknowledge Him in our ways, He promises to direct our
path (see Proverbs 3:5–6). God very simply wants to be asked if
He approves of our plan, and told that if He doesn't, we are happy
to change it. We are instructed in God's Word to

> *Commit to the Lord whatever you do, and he will establish
> your plans.*
>
> Proverbs 16:3 (NIV)

Our plans won't work well unless God blesses them, and very
often He does just that if we submit them to Him. Most of the
details of daily living God leaves to our free choice, but He does
want to be acknowledged.

Scheduling is the art of planning your activities so that you can achieve your goals in the time you have available. Scheduling can maximize your effectiveness and reduce your stress levels.

Lack of scheduling, on the other hand, reduces productivity and results in wasting time instead of enjoying the rewards of a fruitful life and the best that God has for us. We can be proactive instead of reactive—that means we need to take the initiative. A life of reaction is actually a life of bondage. Decide what you want to do each day, before other things and people start making your decisions for you. Just as we have a financial budget of some kind, we need a time budget. A time budget helps us avoid stress and not waste time on less important tasks while running out of time for the important ones.

Don't try to do this on your own, but first commit yourself and your day to the Lord. Offer up all you are and have, including your time, to Him, and ask for His guidance as you plan your day.

When we ask God for direction, we probably won't be given a specific outline of what the day should look like, but we can depend on God to guide us as we schedule and plan our day. God has given us common sense and wisdom as gifts, and as a part of our free will, He expects us to use them in daily planning. Planning is simply thinking wisely. It is looking at how much time you have and deciding what you want or need to do with it.

How much can we realistically get done in one day? What can we accomplish without frustration and stress? What are the most pressing things we need to attend to first? What could we roll into tomorrow if we need to? Is our planning leaving room for us to live a balanced life that includes worship, rest, laughter, as well as accomplishment?

As a recovering workaholic, I must confess that I did not always apply the principles I am encouraging you to apply. I learned by my mistakes, but perhaps you can learn without making the same ones I made.

What unfinished projects do you have that bother you the most when you think about them? It could relieve a lot of stress and therefore give you more energy if you would just systematically start doing them and eliminate the stress they cause. Putting a project off never makes it easier to do later on. Seize it and get it over with!

The very thoughts of planning and, especially, scheduling may cause some people not to want to read another word of this book. Our temperament determines just how detailed we are willing or able to be in things like scheduling. My personal assistant is beyond organized! Her calendar and the copy of mine she keeps and manages are color coordinated with color-coordinated sticky notes covering each month. Each note has a tiny, very neat message. She can put those calendars in front of her and take delight in reading and rereading them and improving them in any way she can for hours at a time. If I decide to change one appointment, something I do quite often, it usually has a ripple effect that can mean she needs to move several other things, and she doesn't seem to mind at all. If I worked for me, I would look at me and say, "You have got to be kidding, Joyce. I just got this thing organized, and now you want to change it?"

I remember asking her once what she liked to do when she had time off and she actually said, "I love to organize!" I thought she was joking, but she wasn't. It is very obvious that her skills are a gift that God has given her, and it is also obvious that I don't have them, so I am glad I have her.

God gives us different gifts and He wants us to use them for one another's benefit. You never have to be like someone else! Although we may not have the type of organizational skills that some people do, we all do have an ability to be organized enough not to waste our life. If you feel that you are lacking in these skills, don't just assume that you are not an organized person, but at least be willing to learn and grow. I also highly recommend you don't say on a regular basis, "I am just not organized." Our words are powerful, and negative words can keep us trapped in a weakness that we would like to be free from.

My daughter, Laura, is admittedly not very organized. She also tends to forget things frequently, but, interestingly enough, she runs an entire household that consists of her husband and three children. In addition to that, she helps take care of my widowed aunt, who is in a nursing home, and she works part time for me. I interviewed her briefly for this book to ask how someone who is disorganized manages to keep up with the things she keeps up with. She shared that making a note each day about what she needs to do that day is the most helpful to her. And then she said, "But even then, I may forget to read my note." Then she added, "Mom, you have no idea how often God reminds me to do something just in the nick of time, and that is what keeps me out of trouble."

So we can see from this that God helps us in our weaknesses. His strength is actually seen through them. Pray, make a plan, and trust God to help you remember to work your plan!

The Spontaneous Person

Some people have an aversion to planning because they say they are spontaneous and they want to be free to do what and when they choose. That, of course, is their right, but I seriously doubt they will do as much good with their time as they would if they included a little planning in their life.

We need a certain amount of spontaneity so we don't become so rigid with our plans and schedules that we don't leave room for anything or anyone other than our own "plan." Doing something on the spur of the moment is good for all of us occasionally. But *occasionally* is the key to not letting it get out of control. I am spontaneous to a degree (most people who know me would probably say to a tiny degree), but before I drop everything and do something spontaneously because a friend or one of my children has asked me to, I have to think about my responsibilities and ask myself if there is anything I have to get done today that I can't put off.

Responsibility, even though it may not always be the most exciting thing, is an important priority. Winston Churchill said, "The price of greatness is responsibility."[12]

Spontaneous people are lots of fun, and we can count on them to be on call for whatever we may want to do, but are they obeying God's original dream for man that they be fruitful? If you are a spontaneous person, don't get angry with me or offended. I am glad that you are you, but if you need a bit of balance or a little shift in priorities, why not read on? No matter what personality you have, the only way you can keep your priorities straight is by being willing to adjust them regularly.

We all have different levels of responsibility in our lives, and if we have accepted the privilege of doing a thing, then we must accept the responsibility. If someone is a doctor, he or she has been given an amazing gift, but with that gift comes the responsibility of being on call and needing to get out of bed in the middle of the night because a patient has been taken to the emergency room. If you want to be the boss, you will have more responsibility than the other employees.

I had the privilege of having four amazing children, but I also had the responsibility that goes along with raising children. No privilege comes without responsibility, and to expect one without the other is plain foolishness.

Making a Plan

We all need a plan for each day. Even if our plan is to do nothing that day, we can still plan it and do it on purpose. The thing I don't want for my life is being manipulated and controlled by circumstances, my own emotions, or other people. If I do a thing, it should be because I have chosen to do it. I hope you want that also. Living my life "on purpose" has become very important to me, and it has brought me into an area where I live with less regret than ever before.

I definitely think we need a plan for each day, but how we do the planning is totally up to us and can certainly accommodate our own temperament. I have lots of plans because that is the way I like to live. I already have planned what I will eat at the restaurant we are going to tonight. I have several friends who tease me a lot about planning where, when, and what I am going to eat, but they also like eating with me because it is almost always good! I planned to go to the restaurant I am going to tonight a week ago and made reservations to be sure I could get in. That way I won't be disappointed.

I planned how many hours I wanted to work today and the phone calls I wanted to make. I plan out my day each morning, but I can adapt most things if I really need to. Without plans we have no direction, and we end up doing nothing, or, at best, very little. We are at the whim of whoever and whatever comes our way. I feel fulfilled right now because it is late in the afternoon and I have accomplished a lot, yet I still have time to relax and do something fun.

Making plans like I am talking about doesn't require complicated planning, it just requires that you do a little thinking about what you want to do with your time. If you do make a plan and it needs to be adjusted, then be flexible, but at least have a plan of some kind.

There is rarely a day when all of my plans work out, or when I don't have to do some things I did not plan, so I even plan for the unexpected to happen. Always leave some room in your schedule for the things you didn't schedule and it will help you avoid stress and pressure. Anyone who thinks his or her day will go perfectly according to his or her plan is sure to be frustrated and disappointed. Recently, I had two days in succession where I didn't accomplish much of what I had planned, but I did end up spending one day with my daughter unexpectedly and another one with Dave. The day after that occurred, I was talking with the Lord and said, "I am frustrated because I didn't accomplish much of what I had planned the past two days," and immediately I heard Him speak in my heart that frustration was a total waste of time and did nothing but make me miserable. Then He reminded me that relationships with my family are very important and that I did use my time wisely after all.

Expect the Unexpected!

As I mentioned previously, it is wise to leave some room in your planning and thinking for the unexpected! One of my self-induced problems for many years was that I didn't leave any room in my schedule for things like that. I planned things literally back-to-back with no time in between, and it was a recipe for stress! I ended up rushing and being angry because people and things got in the way of "my" plan. I am not fond of what I call small bursts of downtime—the ten- and fifteen-minute intervals between things that don't leave me enough time to do anything really worthwhile. I always looked at them as wasted time until I realized I needed those times to breathe and regroup my thoughts. Those are good times to thank God, or just talk with Him about how your day is going. If things are not going well, it may be an opportunity to hear from God about what adjustments you might make to still end up with a fruitful day.

If we leave no time between appointments and things we have committed to do, what happens if the doctor is ten minutes late, we get stuck in unexpected traffic, or we get a last-minute phone call that we cannot resist taking? The answer is pressure happens, and it happens to us! When facing that pressure, we often pass it on to someone else we are dealing with. The simple act of planning some time for things you did not expect could bring a great deal of peace into your world.

If you hoped I would give you a detailed guide of how to plan your day, you will be disappointed. If that is what you want, there are numerous books you can purchase that will give you a step-by-step formula for planning and scheduling. Someone else's formula never works for me, but if it works for you, go for it. I do urge you not to spend your life just wanting to know what others did that works for them, in the process never finding what God has for you. I firmly believe we are individuals, and God will guide us if we will give Him the opportunity. My methods of organizing are not like my administrative assistant's. I don't live by color coordinates and sticky notes, but I do have my own system that works for me.

I believe that if I successfully convey to you the importance of having a plan and disciplining yourself to stick to it within reason, you are wise enough to look at your own life and make some decisions. I believe we need room to breathe rather than being trapped in a formula that has worked for someone else but may never work for us. Spiritual maturity requires that at some point we untie our boat from the dock and give ourselves to the waves of God's Spirit, which is another way of saying: "Learn to be led by the Holy Spirit."

One of the greatest things any Bible teacher can teach you is how to be led by the Holy Spirit. He alone can bring the variety and creativity into our lives that will prevent us from being bored with sameness, rules, and regulations. I challenge you to ask God for a plan for the day, and believe that He will guide you. Now look at what you either need or want to accomplish today (some of both, I hope) and decide what to do first, second, and so on. Some people like lists and others don't, so have fun finding out what works for you. Finding a plan that works for you may require some trial and error.

Let's say you really seriously want to exercise regularly. It may be working out at the gym, walking regularly with a friend, or using a treadmill or some other equipment you can purchase and bring into your home. You sign up at the gym or you buy your equipment and you try getting up an hour earlier than usual and you absolutely hate it. You end up being tired all day, and after a week you abandon your plan and continue making payments to the gym you hope to get to someday. Or you look at the treadmill that now only screams at you that you are not in good shape.

Instead of giving up, try something else. Try working out later or on the weekend or whatever it takes to get you started. Once you get a good start, you will probably find it easier to increase the number of days or the time, but don't give up because your first effort didn't work. After sixty-two years of not working out and living with my "in shape" husband who has exercised diligently since he was a teenager, I finally decided to stop making excuses and do something. I decided that something was better than nothing, even if that something was only fifteen minutes three times a week. Amazingly, now with ten years of successful weight training behind me, I can see clearly why I failed so many years before finding success.

I kept trying plans and programs, thinking I should be able to do what others were doing and be successful overnight, but my thinking was unrealistic. We usually want to get in shape in a couple of weeks, but it won't happen. Plan for a long, long, long, long time, and then you won't be disappointed. I think we are often defeated because the plan we begin with is where someone else has landed after many years of experience.

You can go buy a book giving you details on scheduling and it may help, but keep in mind that it was written by someone who probably failed their way to success before writing the book. Give yourself time and room to be imperfect while you're improving.

> Give yourself time and room to be imperfect while you're improving.

Planned Neglect

Have you ever thought of planning to neglect some things? I think it is a good idea and one that will save time. We can plan to neglect the phone for an hour. Honestly, I never knew I was so important until I got a cell phone with texting and e-mail on it. Suddenly, I think I must be available for the world at all times and act as if things would fall apart if they could not contact me for one hour!

A little planned neglect will help us remember that the world can survive after all if we are not present for an hour. It is sad indeed when we feel that we must take the phone with us when we go to the toilet.

We could neglect answering some of our calls until later. I find that very often if I don't answer, the person calling will leave a text message that requires no answer. I recently told my administrative assistant that I didn't want her to send me any text messages or folders full of business for thirty days, unless it was an emergency. I was recovering from hip surgery and wanted the time to recover peacefully. When the thirty days were over, she said it was amazing how many things worked themselves out within a few days that she would have normally sent to me to deal with. Surprisingly, she didn't have all that much to give me, even after thirty days. Wow! I wasn't as important as I thought I was!

The more we are available, the more people depend on us. We can give others some responsibility by simply planning a little neglect. I am not suggesting we neglect legitimate responsibilities, but we truly don't have to be available to everyone all the time.

A famous violinist shared that she practiced her violin first and purposely planned to neglect everything until that was finished. Then she made her bed, dusted the furniture, answered phone calls, et cetera. No wonder she became famous!

Time management is really self-management. If we don't manage ourselves, our lives can be nothing other than chaotic. Frustrated people usually blame their problems on life, but God doesn't want life to just happen to us; He wants us to subdue and manage it.

Chapter Summary

- Scheduling can maximize your effectiveness and reduce your stress levels.
- Is your planning leaving room for you to live a balanced life that includes worship, rest, and laughter as well as accomplishment?

- Putting a project off never makes it easier to do later on.
- Be organized enough to make the most of your life.
- Pray, make a plan, and trust God to help you work your plan.
- You can actually plan to neglect the things that might distract you and occupy too much of your time.

CHAPTER 11

Following Through with Your Plan

Those who are blessed with the most talent don't neces-sarily outperform everyone else. It is the people with follow-through who excel.

Mary Kay Ash, founder of Mary Kay Cosmetics

Having a plan is the first step to seizing the day, but sticking to the plan is step two, and it is a challenge that we don't always master well. There are probably very few people who have no plan at all. Most of us have something we want to do each day, but the thing that frustrates us is when we come to the end of the day and we know we have been busy all day and yet somehow we didn't accomplish what we set out to do. As a matter of fact, we may not even be sure what we did, but we know that we were busy!

There are many causes for this lack of follow-through, and in this chapter we will deal with three ways to accomplish our goals.

1. Have a "Today Is the Day" Attitude

Having a desire to accomplish something is noble, yet procrasti-nation tempts us and it is very deceptive. When we procrastinate, we never say to ourselves, "I am not going to do this thing I need to do!" We merely tell ourselves that we will do it later, but very often later becomes later and later until the thing never gets done. It is rather natural to want to put off doing less enjoyable things in favor of doing the things we do enjoy, but it is not a character trait of a successful person. Successful people have an ability to stay focused and get the task finished.

We all procrastinate to some degree. I doubt that there is any person on the planet who does everything at the moment it could or should be done, but for some people (I've heard about 20 percent of people) the problem is so severe that it leads to other, even more serious, problems, like passivity and laziness. Procrastination reflects our struggle with self-control.

A person may think he or she is buying time today by procrastinating, but it is like using a credit card. It is fun until you get the bill. The procrastinator will ultimately be confronted with the non-activity and all the problems it has caused.

When we procrastinate, we are in danger of forgetting what we were supposed to do altogether. At times, when I have given someone a task to accomplish and I have to go back to him and ask if it is finished, he says, "I was going to do it but I just have not gotten around to it yet," or "I have been busy, but I am going to do it." That may be the case, but it is also likely that the person procrastinated and then forgot the task completely. If this is the case, then the procrastination led to a bigger problem, which was that the procrasinator didn't tell the truth about why the job wasn't done.

Just Do It!

The famous Nike shirt that carries the saying "Just Do It" is seen around the world. I have been in remote villages in faraway places and seen poor children wearing it. One child, when finally on his way to America, said, "Now I can find out what this saying on my shirt means!" It makes me wonder how many people wear that shirt and have no idea that it is a personal message to them that they are ignoring.

Perhaps you have heard the saying, "The best time to do what needs to be done is now," and that is certainly true. Whether it is paying the bills that are due or picking up the little piece of paper you dropped on the floor—the best time is now! The ability to move oneself to immediate action in dealing with what needs to be done is the trait of a successful person.

> *The ability to move oneself to immediate action in dealing with what needs to be done is the trait of a successful person.*

It is amazing how difficult it is for some people to take action to do some very simple tasks. We use the last of the toilet paper on the roll and when we think about replacing it now, our next thought is *I will do it later.* Later comes, as it always does, and then we or someone else is stuck with going to the bathroom and having no toilet paper. The same thing happens with the last Kleenex in the box, or the last paper towel on the roll. Why don't we just do what needs to be done? No good reason; we just procrastinate because we have never formed a strong habit of doing things as soon as possible! I just walked by the clothes dryer and thought, *I could get the clothes out now and hang them up,* but then I thought, *I will wait until later.* There was absolutely no reason to wait, and, in fact, had I waited I might have forgotten and then found a clothes dryer full of wrinkled clothes that would have created more work, so I decided to follow my own advice and not procrastinate!

This tendency to put things off for no good reason at all must be an inherent trait of the flesh. It is just plain laziness, I suppose, unless it is controlled. No wonder God has given us the fruit of self-control, and if we want to be successful in life we will need to use it numerous times each day (see Galatians 5:22–23).

We subconsciously think that if we do all the things that need to be done now, we won't have time to do the things we want to do, but that isn't true. We will actually have more time to do those things, and we will be able to do them peacefully, without low-level guilt over our procrastination.

I was talking with a man recently and he responded to a question I asked with a giggle and the statement, "Yes, I am a procrastinator." He obviously was not aware of the danger or he would not have giggled! Procrastination is a bad habit, and the best way to overcome it is to form a new habit, a good habit of doing things as soon as possible. Don't waste your time fighting with bad habits, but instead use the biblical principle of overcoming evil with good (see Romans 12:21). Focus on "just doing it," and you will soon be free from procrastination.

2. Dealing with Interruptions Successfully

To interrupt means to stop or hinder by breaking in. For example, "He interrupted the speaker with frequent questions." It means to break the uniformity or continuity of, or to break in upon an action.[13]

I can become easily frustrated when people interrupt me while I am talking (which is most of the time), writing, studying for a sermon, watching a good movie, or talking on the phone. I guess I just don't like to be interrupted! Should we become frustrated with those people and things that interrupt us, or should we find ways to protect ourselves when we are doing things we don't want interrupted?

This morning I was writing and in deep thought when Dave, who was in the kitchen, got a phone call. He was making corrections to an article he had written for our magazine, and I felt mildly irritated because his voice was interrupting my train of thought. I tried to continue for a few minutes, but finally decided I should be the one to take action. So I got up and shut my door. An amazing thing happened: no more interruptions!

We cannot expect the rest of the world to stop functioning because we don't want to be interrupted, so why not be proactive and make arrangements to be where your interruptions will be fewer?

Getting away by yourself to finish a project, or shutting a door, or even telling your family and friends or co-workers that you need not to be interrupted for a specific amount of time could save lots of frustration later. My daughter frequently tells me that she is going in her office without her phone to work on a project and that if I have an emergency I can call her husband or leave a message and she will call me later. She acts proactively, and, by doing so, she avoids interruptions she would surely get if she didn't.

> By prevailing over all obstacles and distractions, one may
> unfailingly arrive at his chosen goal or destination.
>
> Christopher Columbus[14]

Another way to minimize interruptions is to learn to manage them quickly. Don't let yourself be dragged into a problem that you really don't have to solve right now. It is permissible to say no to people if their timing isn't good. When we do get interrupted, the shorter it is, the less long-term damage it will do to our focus. I have had to admit that I often create my own problems by getting involved in things that I truly could stay out of. Someone may interrupt me, but I can quickly deflect it and get right back to what I am focusing on if I choose to, but many times I make a choice that I know isn't the best when I make it, and I get into a discussion about a subject that is going to require much more time than I currently have. Why? Curiosity or perhaps an unbalanced need to be involved may be the culprits, but I am learning to be responsible for some of my loss of time.

> The only way things change is if we take responsibility to change them.

The only way things change is if we take responsibility to change them. In learning how to seize my day and get the most out of my time, I will need to overcome these temptations, and so will you.

We do, of course, need to be able to discern between unnecessary interruptions and God-interruptions. When Jesus came to Martha and Mary's home, Mary stopped what she was doing and sat at His feet to receive teaching. She considered Him not an interruption, but an opportunity she was not going to let pass her by. Martha, on the other hand, didn't stop her work and actually became frustrated because Mary did (see Luke 10:38–42).

Sometimes we make plans and God laughs because He has other plans for us that day that we don't know about yet. Some of the greatest events of all time began in the form of an interruption. Mary was interrupted by an angel with the news that she would give birth to the Savior of the world (see Luke 1:26–31). Saul, who later became the apostle Paul, was on his way to persecute Christians, and he was interrupted by Jesus, who changed his life in an instant (see Acts 9:1–9).

Interruptions at Work

I have heard that the average office worker is interrupted seventy-three times every day, and the average manager is interrupted every eight minutes. Interruptions include telephone calls, incoming e-mail messages or other forms of electronic communication, and interruptions by colleagues and crises. Once there is an interruption it takes an average of twenty minutes to get back to the same level of concentration that we were at prior to disruptions. We can easily spend our entire day dealing with interruptions and get nothing done that we planned to do. We cannot eliminate all interruptions, because some of them are very important.

I think it is polite to form a habit of not interrupting someone who seems deep in thought unless we have no other choice. Perhaps we could write down things we may need to ask the individual and then find a time to ask them all at one time. Perhaps if we sow good seeds of not interrupting others we can reap a harvest of not being interrupted so often ourselves.

Technology has given us many gifts, and among them are dozens of new ways to grab our attention. It is hard to talk to a friend without at least one call coming in on our call-waiting feature. You may check your Facebook or Twitter a couple of times while trying to read a chapter of this book. It is common now when I am teaching in my conferences to have people listening and then texting their friends about comments I have made while teaching. I often wonder how much of what I am saying they miss while texting about the last thing I said!

What is a distraction? Do these types of things qualify and, if so, how do they affect us? Researchers say they are making us dumber. They feel quite certain that all the multitasking is deteriorating our mental capacity. Most of us realize that if we try to do two things at once, they both suffer to some degree, but in today's fast-paced society we continue doing it. It seems as if we are on a treadmill that is going so fast we cannot find a safe place to get off.

Alessandro Acquisti, a professor of information technology, and Eyal Peer, a psychologist at Carnegie Mellon, were commissioned to design an experiment that would measure the brainpower lost when someone deals with interruptions.[15]

The test involved three groups of participants. Group one answered 136 questions with no interruptions. Groups two and three answered the same questions with two interruptions. Then groups two and three were tested again and *told* they would be interrupted. One group was interrupted, but the other group awaited interruptions that never came.

During the initial test where groups two and three received two interruptions, they answered correctly 20 percent less of the time than those who were not interrupted. The group that was retested and once again was interrupted improved by 6 percent, proving that if we experience interruptions that we were expecting, we can learn to deal with them better. The group that was told they would be interrupted but were not improved an amazing 43 percent. They even outperformed the group who had no interruptions. It was concluded that the participants in group three adapted to the interruptions and improved when they had none.

A Stanford sociologist named Clifford Nass, who conducted some of the first tests on multitasking, said, "Those who can't resist the lure of doing two things at once are 'suckers for irrelevancy.'" Some professionals definitely feel that those who are addicted to texting and tweeting are being robbed of brainpower. I guess we won't know for sure until they are a bit older, but by then it may be too late.

What is the solution? I think once again it is balance that keeps us safe. Too much of anything, even a good thing, always becomes a problem. Use technology, but don't let it run your life, or possibly ruin your life. We may need to multitask occasionally, but we don't have to live that way. Some interruptions are part of everyone's life, but we can learn to manage them better.

> *Use technology, but don't let it run your life.*

3. Count the Cost before Committing

Beginning a project does not always require much of us, but following through and finishing it always does. Anyone can have an idea, thought, or plan for something, but only the diligent will be successful (see Proverbs 12:24).

Progress always takes time and commitment. It usually takes more time than we thought it would, and the cost of the commitment is greater than we thought it would be, if we even thought about it at all.

Too many of us start things or commit to be part of something without giving it much forethought. How long will it take? What will I have to give up to do it? What will it cost in money, time, or energy? Will what I get out of it be worth what I will have to put into it? These are all good questions to ask ourselves and think about.

One of the main ways that I have learned what to put my time into in ministry, and what not to put my time into, is to consider whether the fruit I will gain will be equal to the effort I will have to make. Not only do I do this, but we also do it throughout the ministry.

One of the big mistakes an organization or an individual may make is to keep doing something that was valuable at one time but is no longer valuable. Take a fresh look at what you are doing on a regular basis and ask if it is something worth doing.

Making a Commitment to Christ

I believe it is safe to say that one of the greatest needs in the church world today is a greater emphasis on discipleship. Jesus invited people not merely to come to Him, but to follow Him and be His disciple. To be a disciple of anyone, we discipline ourselves to learn his or her ways and follow his or her example.

From the moment people receive Jesus as their Savior, having made the decision to become Christians, it is important that we instruct them concerning the need for discipleship, and let them know that it will require some effort on their part. Our teachings and sermons to God's people should include a great deal of teaching about becoming more and more like Jesus in all of our ways.

Jesus said that if we want to follow Him we need to be willing to persevere and carry our cross (see Luke 14:27). What does it mean to carry our cross? In short, it means that it will cost us some things that we might find difficult to let go of. Things like loss of reputation or friendships. It will cost time and effort, and we will need to be willing to learn, learn, and then learn some more. Being a disciple is about much more than simply going to church and having a fish emblem on your car.

The devil doesn't mind all that much if you go to church, as long as you don't learn much about discipleship. He doesn't want people to be saved, but if they are, he really doesn't want them to become like Jesus.

Jesus told a story to help those who intended to follow Him realize what they would need to do. He said if a man intended to build a building, he would first calculate the cost to see whether he had sufficient means to finish it (see Luke 14:28).

One of our daughters and her husband were once in the process of beginning to build a new home. They spent at least six months talking about it and thinking about it. They decided what they thought they could afford to build and sought out proper designs. They searched for a good builder and starting getting bids on what it would cost to finish it. As people often find, the cost was much higher than they had intended to pay. Then they had to decide if they wanted to build their home the way they'd planned, make it smaller and not quite as nice as they wanted, or not build it at all. When they decided they wanted it the way they planned it, they had to decide if they could, and were willing to shift other things in their life in order not to be under financial pressure to build it. They did all of this before they signed papers making a commitment to do it.

Whether you want to build a house, lose weight, get out of debt, get a college degree, clean the closet, or anything else, count the cost! Ask yourself enough questions to be realistic about what it will take to do it; otherwise you will make a plan and then not follow through!

Chapter Summary

- Self-control is an essential fruit of the Spirit to have in order to finish what you start.
- The best way to correct a bad habit is to form a good habit.
- Take action instead of procrastinating.
- Be proactive and make arrangements that will help limit interruptions.
- We should count the cost before making a commitment.
- Balance in life is important. Too much of anything, even a good thing, can become a problem.
- Beginning a thing is easy—following through takes perseverance.

CHAPTER 12

Organization

For every minute spent organizing, an hour is earned.

Author Unknown

Organizing is important to do before we embark on a project. We may have a plan, a schedule, and we may be determined, but if we are not organized before we begin, it will cost us a lot of time.

Benjamin Franklin said, "A place for everything and everything in its place."[16] When I have a project, which for me is usually writing books or preparing sermons, once I get an idea, I want to get started on it right away. But I am still learning that some time spent organizing will save me time later. One thing that is important for me to do is gather all the resources I will more than likely use, so I don't have to interrupt my thoughts to get up and find a book I need for reference material.

The things I intend to use should be organized around me and easy to get to so I don't waste time reaching for things that are out of reach, accidently knocking things on the floor and having to clean up messes. Once I am settled in my chair and have my computer on my lap and other things balanced around me, I don't want to get up. I have had more than one occasion when I have needed something that was just beyond my reach and, while trying to stretch to get it, I have knocked over my coffee or a pile of books. Cleaning up the mess takes more time than I would have spent if I had organized better to begin with.

I have had many times when I have gotten into my recliner where I pray and study and had to get up to find my glasses, then get up again to get Kleenex, and then go find my pen, and then realize I left my phone in the bathroom downstairs. I sit in my chair and yell as loud as I can for Dave, hoping he will hear me and bring it up, but it rarely works out. Once I am in a recliner with a furry cover over me, I am not interested in getting out, but my disorganization demands that I do it anyway. Think of the time and stress I would have saved by taking a few moments to gather everything I needed before I sat down.

If a busy mom is going to clean her home, she should organize her cleaning supplies and have them close at hand. I was staying in a condo recently and a woman was sent to clean and I noticed she had a rolling tote with everything in it that she would need, and she simply took it along with her. She never had to go "find" things before she could do the work she came to do.

We can waste a lot of time going to find things that we need for a project, but, even more importantly, when we break our concentration there is always a temptation to lose focus and waste even more time.

If a mechanic is going to work on an automobile, he needs to have all of his tools close at hand, and they should be kept in good working condition. There are countless examples like this, but the reality is the same: organization saves time and disorganization wastes it!

Organization saves time and disorganization wastes it!

We call businesses "organizations." Many Web addresses end

with the well-known tag *.org*. These titles may have just become phrases to us, but they are intended to mean something. The message is, "I have something to offer through my business and I am organized and ready to provide it."

I have always been intrigued by a scripture in the Bible that reads "A dream comes with much business and painful effort" (Ecclesiastes 5:3 AMPC).

Success in life requires a goal, a plan, determination, and organization. One may start a business, but certain disciplines need to be in place if it is to succeed. We have a successful ministry, and we are reaching out to hurting people around the world, but it takes a huge amount of organization to be able to do it. We make plans, and we have schedules, processes, and organization that lead us to good results. A dream by itself never comes to pass. Your dream can become your nightmare if you don't realize you need hard work, order, and organization to see it become a reality. I have met people who are extremely frustrated because they have a goal that is not being reached. Close examination always reveals that they have more "wishbone than backbone." That means that they want to have a good end result, but they don't want to put out the effort needed to make it happen!

Your dream can become your nightmare if you don't realize you need hard work, order, and organization to see it become a reality.

Dreams come to pass with much business and painful effort. A home is not built on a wish, good parenting must be more than a wish, and good health is more than a wish. Start with a dream and then add the things that will bring it to pass. Organization is one of those things.

Clutter

When clutter in the home or office begins mounting, our stress and frustration rise along with it: magazines piled on tables, too many knickknacks, a dirty coffeepot, trash that overflows, and dust covering everything! There is a popular television show called *Hoarders*. These are people who cannot get rid of anything, and eventually their homes are complete disasters, as well as being unsanitary. Not only can they not get rid of anything, they also collect and purchase all kinds of things, and many of them for no reason except to have them.

This is disorganization to an extreme that would be considered a psychological problem that needs professional help. These people have to hire a firm that comes in and brings order once again by getting rid of the clutter. Most of us will never need to go to that extreme to get organized, but if anyone has let things get so far out of hand that they can't even imagine trying to correct it, then getting some help would be wise.

I am more likely to get rid of things I am finished with or no longer using, but Dave is a keeper of things. He has a large collection of various-sized bags, for example. A few days ago someone gave me a beautiful candle that was fairly large, and after unpacking it, I headed to the trash with the box it was in. Dave spotted the box and immediately decided it was too nice to throw away, so he kept it.

In his defense, let me say that he is organized with his collections, and for that I am very glad. He keeps his things on shelves or in drawers, and as long as they are out of sight, I can deal with it. Of course, when I need a bag or a box, he always reminds me that if he had not kept it, I would not have what I needed when I needed it.

I once heard that 84 percent of Americans who experience regular stress said that the disorganization of their homes was an underlying cause. They worried because their homes were not clean enough and well organized. The main culprit was clutter.

Clutter makes me feel confused, so I get rid of things I am not using. I highly recommend taking a look around your home and cleaning out things that are merely taking up space but are not being used. Most of us have plastic containers with lids in our home for storing food items. Mine are at the point where when I open the cabinet they are in, they start falling out. The lids are not with the right containers and while trying to find the ones I need I usually get frustrated. It is time to go through them, get rid of the ones I rarely use, and put the lids and containers together that go together. A few moments to organize will save me a great deal of time in the long run.

My daughter recently told me that she fights with clutter all the time. She has three teenagers who constantly bring things into the house, dropping them in any convenient space and then becoming frustrated when they don't know where they left them.

If you have an active household with several people living in it, I admit that organization will be more difficult and your "organized household" might look different than the home of someone who lives alone or just with their spouse. However, we all need some form of organization if we intend to get anything done.

The best way to keep things organized is to implement small daily routines that will, over time, result in a better-kept environment. It is also wise to make sure that everyone in the household is doing his or her part. Many parents struggle with this, but the best thing to do is to train children when they are young to pick up after themselves. If you do everything for them when they are little, you will more than likely still be doing it as they get older.

If you think it is already too late, don't just give up. It is never too late for a new beginning in any area of life. Even if you have a problem, don't keep adding to it by continuing the same bad habits that created it to begin with.

Most of the things you get rid of to declutter your home will never be missed. It probably will help you enjoy the things you keep more. I have noticed that if I have too many things on a table that are intended to decorate it, I end up not really enjoying any particular item that I thought was so lovely when I purchased it. Less is often better!

It is sometimes difficult to get rid of things that people have given us. Even if we have no use for them and don't even like them, we may feel obligated to keep them. After all, if they ask us about them we don't want to say we don't have it any longer. I have had to take the stance that if you give me something it is mine to do with as I please, and even if I give it away, that is my choice. I sincerely believe that God provides some things for us as "seed to sow." They were intended to pass through our hands to someone else. My son David and I laugh often about the gift he gave me one year for Christmas that I gave back to him two years later as a gift. I didn't do it on purpose, but when I received it, I knew I would never use it, so it went into what I call my "giveaway box." Having forgotten who gave it to me, I later tried to give it to him. We had a good laugh when he said, "Mom, I gave you this!"

Find a plan or system that works for you, and consistently eliminate as much clutter as possible. You will be amazed at the calming effect it has on your environment. I believe that chaos hinders my creativity. It may not have that effect on everyone, but it does on me.

Wasting Time Looking for What You Didn't Put Away

We all know the frustration of looking for our car keys when it is time to leave and not being able to find them or looking for our phone and having to have someone call it to help us locate it. If no one else is home we are on our own and if you are like me, you often find items in really weird places. I have put my phone with my makeup and closed it up in a drawer. I have left it in my shoe rack while choosing shoes for the day. I have even had it in my hand while frantically running around the house trying to find it. Benjamin Franklin's advice for everything to have a place and to put everything in its place is good advice.

In order for this to happen, we will have to slow down. The speed at which we live is the main reason we don't take time to put things away. Organization requires thought, and that requires time. Once we get too busy to think in an organized way, we are surely on our way to having big problems eventually.

A large part of our problem is having a schedule that is so busy it eats away at our sanity. In our modern society, most of us are too busy and we have too much stuff! Most of us have more clothes in our closet that we don't wear than those that we do. Let's be honest: How many pairs of shoes do you own and which ones do you actually wear? I started to go count mine to give you an example, but I decided it might be too shocking.

How many pairs of earrings do you have and how many of them have you perhaps never had on? I went through all my cabinets recently, including my china cabinet, and found beautiful bowls and platters that I didn't even remember! I am trying to make a commitment to use things if I am going to keep them.

God's Word urges us to be prudent (see Proverbs 13:16). Prudence is good management of our resources. We should use the things we have, because if we don't we are wasting them. There is someone somewhere who will use what is merely collecting dust in our homes, so let's pass these items on.

Health Benefits of Being Organized

I once read an article that talked about the health benefits of being organized. Here are some of the things I learned:

1. Organization reduces financial stress

Excessive stress always has an adverse effect on our health and should be avoided. Financial stress is one type of stress that takes its toll on us. If, due to a lack of organization, you misplace bills, have to pay late fees, and repurchase items that you cannot find, the costs add up quickly. Financial stress is one of the major causes of marital problems. The Bible says that a wise man knows the state of his flocks. For us that means he knows how much money he has and what he is doing with it. He knows when his bills are due, and he pays them early or on time. Just think of the stress it causes when you get a credit card bill you failed to pay and now realize seventy-five dollars has been added in interest that you could have avoided had you been more organized.

What if a person does not plan well for his year-end taxes that will come due? Some people want all the money they can get from their paychecks, so they fail to have enough taxes deducted throughout the year. Others may be self-employed and have the responsibility of making sure that they set aside enough out of their profits to pay their taxes. Yet many don't do that, and when the end of the year comes, they panic and their stress level is high. It is not their taxes causing their stress; their poor planning and

> *Better organization always equals less stress.*

lack of organization are the culprits. Better organization always equals less stress.

2. Organization minimizes personal conflicts

If relationships are strained due to arguments over lost items, missed appointments, bills not paid on time, forgotten errands, and clutter, it can cause serious problems in a marriage. This is especially the case if a very organized person marries someone who is extremely disorganized. An organized person can be too rigid in his or her expectations and might need to adjust, but a disorganized person can cause a lot of frustration, and he or she will have to find ways to improve. I actually know of a couple who ended up getting divorced because of the constant conflict that was caused by a similar situation.

A disorganized person cannot be depended on to follow through with tasks, and the trust is eroded in a marriage when this happens. We need to be able to depend on those we are in relationships with.

3. Organization increases "me" time

When we are organized it leaves time to do the things we really enjoy. Like exercise (yes, some people actually like it) or a painting class or reading. However, if we never have time for those things, we soon begin to feel deprived, and that creates resentment. If these feelings are present for a long time, they will eventually create other bad attitudes and problems.

We are intended to live well-balanced lives, but that is not possible without good organization skills.

4. Organization helps us have a better diet

Many people have very poor eating habits and they say they don't have time to prepare the foods that are healthy. They eat a lot of fast food or prepackaged foods that are stripped of a lot of the needed nutrition. They don't even have time to purchase and take vitamins. Is it possible that a little more organization could give us time to be healthier? I think it is entirely possible, and I believe eating well should be a greater priority.

I urge you to pray and find a way to be organized. Don't waste any more of your time being frustrated about a problem that you can do something about if you choose to. Don't use the one life you have never doing the things you believe are important. Make whatever changes you need to make, reclaim your life, and be the person you were meant to be!

Chapter Summary

- Getting organized before you start a project will save you time in the long run.
- In order to succeed in life, you need a goal, a plan, determination, and organization.
- The best way to keep things organized is to implement small daily routines that will, over time, result in a better-kept environment.
- Chaos hinders creativity.
- It is never too late for a new beginning in any area of life.
- Organization relieves stress!

CHAPTER 13

What Are You Living For?

More men fail through lack of purpose than lack of talent.
                                            Billy Sunday

Earlier I said that we should use our free will to choose the will of God. Part of His purpose for us is that we live "on purpose" for a purpose. Many people feel useless, and they waste their time wondering why they are on earth. "Who am I? What am I here for?" is the cry of many hearts.

You are here because God wants you! You are important to Him, and you fit into His purposes. You are not an accident. You are personally designed by the hand of God and have been given abilities that you are to use in the service of God and man.

One of our downfalls is that we compare ourselves, and what we can or cannot do, with other people. That is a huge mistake. God will never help you be anyone other than you! I think self-acceptance is vital if we intend to go on to find our purpose in life. In addition to loving God, fellowshipping with Him, and becoming a disciple of Jesus who is being molded into His image, we each have a part to play in the plan of God for the redemption of man.

Get to know yourself and learn to appreciate yourself! Every day that you are against yourself is another day that you waste. It is important to be able to say, "I like myself, and I love myself with the love of God." To do anything other than that is to offend God. I once heard a pastor tell a woman who had just said that she hated herself, "Who do you think you are? If God loved you enough to send His Son to die for you, surely you can stop hating yourself and become useful to God."

Just because I may not be the person I would have liked to be does not mean that I am not exactly what God wants me to be. I may not be behaving exactly the way He would like me to, but our behavior improves as we learn the Word of God and develop a strong relationship with Him. God loves us while we are changing just as much as He will once we have changed!

> God loves us while we are changing just as much as He will once we have changed!

Until we have a deep understanding of God's love for us, and the right standing we have with Him through our faith in Jesus, we will never have an improvement in our behavior. God accepts you, and He will never reject you.

I would have liked to have been able to sing like some people do or play a musical instrument or paint, but God didn't give me those gifts, so obviously I was not supposed to be a singer, a musician, or a painter. Wasting your life trying to be something that you are not and never will be is useless! God's Word teaches us that it is better to enjoy what is available to us than to live with cravings and wandering desires (see Ecclesiastes 6:9).

One of the best ways that you can stop wasting time is to accept yourself as God designed you this very moment. Don't ever fight against yourself again. Say, "I am what I am, and I cannot do anything God has not designed me to do—but I *can* do everything He has purposed for me. I accept myself as God's creation. He loves me and has a purpose for my life." Even if you don't know what that purpose is yet, this will help you get on your way to discovering it.

Relax and know that because you are alive, you have a purpose. I believe God will use us daily if we ask Him to. There are many things that God does through us, and we never even realize what is happening. I was in the grocery store not long ago and a woman recognized me and got teary-eyed. She said, "Today is my birthday and running into you is my gift from God." I was in the grocery store getting some groceries and God used me to bless someone! I wonder how many times God uses you in some way and you just don't recognize it for what it is.

We may give someone a simple compliment without being aware of how much he or she needed it. You smile at someone and she is comforted because she has just been through a stressful ordeal. That person is encouraged, and we have fulfilled God's purpose for us at that moment. You will miss God's purpose for you if you only look for major world-changing things or things that cause everyone to clap and cheer. God uses small things as much as big things, and sometimes He even uses them more. Always remember that what seems small and insignificant to us may be a life-changing event for someone else!

Seasons of Life

Even when we seek God for a better understanding of His will for us, we may not get a blueprint for the rest of our life. But if we truly want to do God's will, we can trust Him to guide us into it one day at a time. I worked at many jobs before any thought ever came to me that I was to teach God's Word. Each of these jobs was right at the time, because it wasn't time yet for me to do what

God ultimately had in mind for me. God may have to spend the
first half of our lives getting us into position for the second half.

Moses was called to lead the Israelites out of bondage and slavery from Egypt, but for forty years he was raised in Pharaoh's
palace, and for another forty years he lived in the wilderness as a
shepherd, and then God appeared to him and gave him specific
instructions. The first eighty years of his life helped prepare him
for the remainder of it.

The Bible states in Ecclesiastes 3:1 (AMPC) that "to everything
there is a season, and a time for every matter or purpose under
heaven." We can see the seasons of Moses' life and how some of
them may have seemed useless but in reality were not. All of the
time Moses spent in Egypt and the wilderness, he was becoming
the man God needed him to be.

Our grown children play vital roles at Joyce Meyer Ministries. I
had to raise them before they could do that, so God didn't give us
the ministry until three of them were teenagers and we only had
one baby at the time. As the ministry grew and our children grew
into adulthood, God's purpose for all of us became clear. I was
forty-two years old when Joyce Meyer Ministries was birthed, but
obviously God didn't think I was too old to begin. Prior to that,
I wouldn't have been ready for the responsibility I was about to
take on.

Don't despise where you are now or be confused about it. The
Bible says, "Do not despise these small beginnings" (Zechariah
4:10 NLT). Pray and ask God to guide you into His purposes for
your life and then bloom each place that you are planted. Let
the experience you gain now educate you for the next place God
guides you. Some people are so frustrated about finding their
purpose in life that no matter where they are or what they are

doing, they are miserable. Enjoy where you are on the way to where you are going!

Be available for God's use at any time and for any assignment. It doesn't matter if you are the president of the company or a window washer, as long as you are in God's will for the present time.

Living for More than Money and Fame

Many people waste their life seeking money, power, and fame, and yet even if they succeed they still aren't fulfilled and satisfied. All you need to do is to read biographies of wealthy, famous people, and you quickly learn that very few of them truly lived a happy life.

I think the main reason why so many people seek these things is that they are insecure and want to feel important. They don't truly understand that they are already important and valuable because God loves them and has a purpose for them; He planned them and He wants them. What they are looking for cannot be purchased or won at an award ceremony; it can only come from God!

Anyone with true confidence has nothing to prove! A person can have fame and fortune, but his or her worth and value are not rooted in them. Although fame and fortune are nice to have, if a person didn't have them, he or she could still find a way to live life with purpose and pleasure.

Anyone with true confidence has nothing to prove!

When it comes to living a life you can be satisfied with, and one that fulfills you, money and fame alone won't provide it. Wisdom is found in knowing that you aren't working for earthly things alone but are storing up treasure in heaven. Wisdom teaches us to "number our days," reminding us that this earthly life is short and now is the time to follow God. Now is the time to adjust our priorities in such a way that we are putting our energies into the things that truly matter most.

Solomon is said to have been the wisest person who ever lived. When he prayed for wisdom, he asked God to help him discern between good and evil. When we pray for wisdom, we are praying for God to show us the best choice—His best—for our lives. Money and fame are fleeting. The world's financial structure can collapse in a day. In 1929 the stock market crashed and suddenly America was in a depression. In 2008 the stock market fell almost seven thousand points in one day and suddenly what people had invested in the stock market was worth half of what it was when they got up that day.

> In the blink of an eye wealth disappears, for it will sprout wings and fly away like an eagle.
>
> Proverbs 23:5 (NLT)

If we are living only for money—if money is our security—then that kind of news can be very frightening. Enjoy the money you have and use it to help others, but don't make it the source of your confidence.

What about fame? Even if the entire world knows and admires us, history shows that it can forget us very quickly. Most people want to ride the wave of enthusiasm over whoever is the most popular at the time. Whatever we might be famous for is only for a season, and someone better always comes along, and suddenly the world is no longer watching us.

Dave watches a lot of sports, and he is always telling me who the world champion is, or who the best in the world is in one sport or another. But this regularly changes. One person has his season of fame, and he fades away as someone else takes his place. He just told me that someone set a new record in golf, and a few days later he told me someone set a new record in baseball. Someone is always setting new records that top the last ones, so it is unwise to live our lives for fame that is historically proven to be fleeting!

> We will do better in life if we desire to be useful rather than rich and famous.

Once again, let me say that if we have money or fame, it is not a bad thing, but it doesn't have to be what we live for. We will do better in life if we desire to be useful rather than rich and famous.

> *The purpose of life is not to be happy. It is to be useful, to be honorable, to be compassionate, to have it make some difference that you have lived and lived well.*
>
> Ralph Waldo Emerson[17]

Once we discover our gift or talent, the next thing we need to do is give it away. Use your resources in the service of God and man (see Genesis 1:28). We mistakenly think that getting something fulfills us, but it is exactly the opposite. We are only truly fulfilling our purpose and living for the right thing when we are reaching out to give something. I encourage you to deposit into the lives of other people regularly, for if you only make withdrawals you will soon be bankrupt in every way. Live "on purpose" for a purpose!

Peter Drucker said, "There is nothing so useless as doing efficiently that which should not be done at all."

Are you living to make a difference? Do you want the world to miss you when you are gone? How do you want to be remembered? The decisions you make now will determine how the answers to those question turn out.

John W. Gardner, founding chairman of Common Cause, said, "It's a rare and high privilege to help people understand the difference they can make— not only in their own lives, but also in the lives of others, simply by giving of themselves."[18]

Gardner tells of a cheerful old man who asked the same question of just about every acquaintance he fell into conversation with: "What have you done that you believe in and you are proud of?"

He never asked conventional questions such as "What do you do for a living?" It was always "What have you done that you believe in and are proud of?"

It was an unsettling question for people who had built their self-esteem on their wealth or their family name or their exalted job title.

He was delighted by a woman who answered, "I'm doing a good job raising three children," and by a cabinetmaker who said, "I believe in good workmanship and practice it," and by a woman who said, "I started a bookstore and it's the best bookstore for miles around."

"I don't really care how they answer," said the old man. "I just want to put the thought into their minds.

"They should live their lives in such a way that they can have a good answer. Not a good answer for me, but for themselves. That's what's important."

Part of the reason for me writing this book is to help you make decisions that you can be proud of. Nothing is worse than getting up daily, shuffling through the day, and then going to bed in the evening with the empty and frustrated feeling that we have wasted yet another day and have no true idea of what we are living for.

Nothing is more disturbing than watching someone waste his or her life. I know, because I watched my father, mother, and brother waste theirs in different ways. They seemed to be trapped in a place that blinded them to the reality of how empty their lives were. They never grasped the truth concerning the amazing life that they could have had with God. They all believed in God and accepted Christ before they died, but they died having never truly lived.

I did what I could to urge them to make different choices but to no avail, and what I finally realized is that each one of us must decide for ourselves what we want to do with the one life that we have. No one can make us do the right thing. Not even God will force us—He gives us opportunity, but we must choose!

I think the only people we truly remember in life are those who used their lives to help or bless others in some way. I doubt that there is any truly important reason we can find to live merely for ourselves. If we are not living our lives to make someone else's better, then we are not really living at all. Therefore, let me ask one final time: *What are you living for?*

> *If we are not living our lives to make someone else's better, then we are not really living at all.*

Chapter Summary

- God wants you to live "on purpose" for a purpose.
- Self-acceptance is vital to finding your purpose in life.
- God accepts you—He will never reject you.
- An act that seems small and insignificant to you may be a life-changing event for someone else.
- Enjoy where you are on the way to where you are going.
- You are only truly fulfilling your purpose when you are reaching out to help others.
- Each one of us must decide for ourselves what we want to do with the one life that we have.

CHAPTER 14

Being an "On-Purpose" Person

Jesus is the best example of an "on-purpose" person. He came for a purpose, and He purposed to fulfill His purpose. Just look at this example in the book of Luke:

> And when daybreak came, He left [Peter's house] and went into an isolated [desert] place. And the people looked for Him until they came up to Him and tried to prevent Him from leaving them.
> But He said to them, I must preach the good news (the Gospel) of the kingdom of God to the other cities [and towns] also, for I was sent for this [purpose].
>
> Luke 4:42–43 (AMPC)

Jesus had been visiting and preaching in Capernaum, and it was time for Him to go on to another place, but the people tried to prevent Him from leaving. His response informed them that He had to stick to His purpose. Well-meaning people who care about us are often used to prevent us from fulfilling our purpose in life. Their plans are based on what would be best for them, but rarely is that in accord with God's plan.

Jesus came to teach the Gospel, to pay for our sins through His suffering and death (see Hebrews 9:26), to destroy the works of the devil (see I John 3:8), to give us an example to live by (I Peter 2:21), to be an example of serving (Mark 10:45), and to fulfill the Law (Matthew 5:17–18), among other things.

Jesus spent forty days in the wilderness being tempted by the devil, who was tirelessly trying to move Jesus away from His divine purpose (see Luke 4:1–13). Thankfully, Jesus was determined to do the will of God.

At another time, Peter tried to prevent Jesus' purpose by telling Him that He must not go to Jerusalem to suffer at the hands of the Jews. Jesus wasted no time in confronting Peter and telling him that he was a hindrance and a snare. Jesus then said, "Get behind Me, Satan!" (Matthew 16:23). Wow! Talk about dealing with a temptation in a straightforward manner! Jesus knew that Satan was using Peter to try to get Him out of God's will and purpose, and Jesus was determined that would not happen.

The apostle Paul experienced the same type of opposition, and he said that if he had been trying to please people he would not have become an apostle of Jesus Christ (see Galatians 1:10). I know for sure that had I been trying to please people I wouldn't be in ministry today. I wouldn't be writing this book right now. I would probably be frustrated and unfulfilled, wondering why I couldn't seem to find happiness and peace. Most people have no idea the price they will pay if they live to please people instead of living to please and follow God.

It is very clear in Scripture that in the midst of opposition we must determine whether we will choose to please God or people as we travel through life. If we make the right choice now, we will avoid living with regrets later on.

Be Ready for Change

The men who followed Jesus all had careers and were busy, but when Jesus said, "Follow Me," they immediately left what they were doing and followed Him.

What if they had not followed their hearts, but instead had leaned on their own reasoning? They could have missed being part of the greatest miracle in the world. Don't miss your moment! Don't miss your miracle!

They didn't ask what the pay would be, or where they would sleep, or what the workday would look like. Like Abraham when God called him, they went without troubling their minds about where they would go. Abraham is a good example of how we should respond to God's call:

> [Urged on] by faith Abraham, when he was called, obeyed
> and went forth to a place which he was destined to receive
> as an inheritance; and he went, although he did not know or
> trouble his mind about where he was to go.
>
> Hebrews 11:8 (AMPC)

All of these men took risks! If we are not willing to risk what we have now, we will never find out what we could have. I am not suggesting we do foolish things, but if we really think about what these men did, surely they must have appeared foolish to any thinking, reasoning person. However, they were urged on by faith, and faith will take you places where reason would not allow you to go. Living by faith requires us to take a step without always knowing positively what will happen.

> *If we are not willing to risk what we have now, we will never find out what we could have.*

I was busy being a housewife and mom when God called me to teach His Word. In fact, I was making my bed. From that moment I have passionately pursued that purpose. I have had to take many risks, and there have been sacrifices along the way, but I am so grateful that I made the right choice. Unless we fulfill our God-ordained purpose, we will always be searching for something and never attaining it. We end up empty inside and frustrated, but it doesn't have to be that way.

Faith may require us to let go of some things. Many people are fearful of giving up what they feel is safe, but with God, we can be safe in the midst of risk! As long as He is guiding our steps, we are not in danger.

Passionate Pursuit

To be passionate means to be compelled to do a thing by strong, intense feelings. I mentioned that I have pursued one main purpose with passion. But in order to have passion, we must enjoy what we do. I want to do what I am doing—I love it and cannot imagine doing anything else. I suggest that you ask yourself what you love, what you enjoy, and what makes you feel alive. It is difficult to give your life to anything unless you are passionate about it.

I don't believe a loving God would have me do something all of my life that I despised doing. Some people may pursue careers simply because they pay big money, and yet they are miserable all of their lives. May I suggest that money isn't as important as joy and enjoyment! Do something you enjoy! This doesn't mean to live selfishly. Don't get true joy confused with entertainment.

Another thing to ask when searching for your purpose in life is, *What am I good at?* God wants you to succeed, but you won't do that if you are trying to do something that you simply are not good at. I am good at talking. I am a gifted communicator and that makes me comfortable while fulfilling my purpose.

If you love to cook, maybe you should own a restaurant or a catering business. Or maybe you should just cook for your family and friends. If you love to bake, maybe you should start a bakery. I know one woman who absolutely loves to clean house, and she is welcome to come and clean mine anytime she is looking for some enjoyment!

It makes me sad to watch people go through life miserable because they deeply dislike what they are doing. Don't be afraid to make a change, or take a risk. You never know what you may find on the other side of what you think is "safe." Find something that you can be committed to and do it with all of your heart.

Passion keeps us going even in times when we want to give up. Building anything requires a lot of courage and sacrifice, and there are times when we wonder if it is worth it. If we have true passion, we cannot quit even if we want to. Passion takes us across the finish line of our race in life.

> Passion keeps us going even in times when we want to give up.

You might say that a momma bear is passionate about keeping her cubs safe, so she becomes fierce when anyone tries to take them away from her or harm them in any way. Passion makes us fierce in the spirit. It gives us a determination that not everyone understands. We refuse to let our destiny be stolen from us when we have true godly passion.

The Merriam-Webster dictionary partially defines passion as the suffering that Christ endured between the night of the Last Supper and His death.[19] Wow! What a thought. Passion means that we have a willingness to suffer in order to fulfill our purpose.

Jesus suffered, and we have all benefited—that gives Him continual joy. I can say with certainty that if each of us fulfills the purpose for which we are here, we will have joy, and someone else will benefit greatly from our choices in life.

Enthusiasm

Passion is enthusiastic, creative, and alive—it is active! Enthusiasm doesn't just happen, but it is a result of being active in something. I don't feel enthusiastic when I first wake up, so I have to stir myself up. The whole point of being an "on-purpose" person is that we don't live by feeling, but we make choices that we know will give good results, and we invite our feelings to go along if they want to. Most days my feelings get on board and go along with me, but there are some days when they don't. Those are testing days, and we grow spiritually and we develop character on those days.

I wake up in the morning and, most days, before getting out of bed I declare that something good is going to happen to me that day and that something good will happen through me. I pray for and expect the day to be blessed. I pray for energy, enthusiasm, zeal, and passion—and then I get up!

Don't start your day feeling guilty about the mistakes and failures of yesterday. Receive God's mercy and forgiveness and expect good things to happen to you and through you. If you feel badly about yourself, it will drain your energy and that won't help you seize today and make it count.

It is important that you start your day right, and making sure you don't have a bad attitude toward yourself is part of doing that. How we feel about ourselves affects all of our actions. If we devalue ourselves and feel worthless, it will adversely affect how we interact with other people. The fact that Jesus died for you gives you infinite worth and value. Believe that you are important to God's plan and you will be more enthusiastic about facing the day.

By the time I begin my day like this, I am feeling pretty enthusiastic about getting started. This is an important part of my "on-purpose" day. I spend time with God because I know the day will not go right if I don't, but mostly I do it because I love Him and I want to be with Him. During that time I often think over what I need or want to accomplish that day and then I get started!

You might be thinking that all you need to do is clean house today and that you surely cannot be enthusiastic about that, but you actually can! If you get your day started right, you will be surprised by how many things you can enjoy and do with a bounce in your step.

A positive mind leads to an energetic, enthusiastic life!

> *A positive mind leads to an energetic, enthusiastic life!*

Don't Waste Today

I challenge you not to waste today! Live it fully and do it on purpose. God's glory is man fully alive! I talk to one or more of my children every day unless I am out of the country and in a strange time zone. I can usually tell by the tone of their voices what kind of day they are having. If I say, "How are you today?" and they answer in a low tone, "I guess I am okay," I am always disappointed because I know something is bothering them and I want my children to fully enjoy each day they have. How could God feel any less about His children?

We all go through things, and not every day is going to be perfect, but let's make a decision to enjoy and fully live each day that God gives us. Make your days count, because time goes by faster than most of us can imagine. I told my children the other day that we should laugh as much as possible and make memories together, and they agreed.

Don't just drift through life. Don't live in darkness, but follow the light as Jesus taught us to do.

> So Jesus said to them, You will have the Light only a little while longer. Walk while you have the Light [keep on living by it], so that darkness may not overtake and overcome you. He who walks about in the dark does not know where he goes [he is drifting].
>
>   John 12:35 (AMPC)

If we don't purposely follow the light, the darkness will overtake us. I think for our purposes in this book, we can say that following the light refers to doing what we know is the right thing to do. As long as we are purposely engaged in doing what is right, the darkness cannot overtake us. It has no power over us. But if we drift along with no purpose, we will be deceived by the darkness.

Chapter Summary

- Jesus is the best example to follow as you strive to live an "on-purpose" life.
- We all have a choice to make—will we live to please other people or will we live to please God?
- Faith will take you places where reason would not allow you to go.
- Give your life to that thing you are passionate about doing.
- Enthusiasm isn't just a feeling—enthusiasm is a choice.
- The fact that Jesus died for you gives you infinite worth and value.

CHAPTER 15

Activity and Passivity

Then said the Lord to me, You have seen well, for I am alert and active, watching over My word to perform it.

Jeremiah 1:12 (AMPC)

God describes Himself as alert and active, and since we are created in His image (see Genesis 1:27) and told to imitate Him (see Ephesians 5:1), it is reasonable to assume that we can also be alert and active.

Activity is the exact opposite of passivity. Adam was passive in the Garden of Eden when Eve gave him the forbidden fruit; without any opposition to her suggestion, he ate it. God had given Adam an instruction not to eat fruit from that particular tree, and He had also told him that if he did eat of it, the result of his disobedience would be severe. God also gave Adam authority and the power of choice, but when Adam was tempted to make the wrong choice, he did not use his authority to resist it.

The fallout from Adam's passivity, which led to his sin, not only hurt him, but it caused a problem for all of mankind that could have been avoided. Adam very simply did not use his free will to choose the will of God in this situation. Although he knew what God's will was, he allowed his emotion to lead him in following his wife.

Passivity is non-action or non-resistance. The passive person is led by feelings more than by following the leading of the Holy Spirit. Passive people have free will, or the power of choice, but they don't use it, and the problems their passivity leads to are too great to be calculated accurately. One definition of passivity that I have heard is "receiving suffering without resistance," and that is exactly what passive, inactive people are doing, even though they may not realize it at the time. They end up suffering in many different ways and they just blame it on a variety of things, none of which are the real problem.

The result of their inactivity shows itself in a life that they do not enjoy, and one that in fact makes them miserable, but rarely do they connect the dots and accept the responsibility for their unpleasant situation. Inactivity is "idleness, or habitual idleness; want of action or exertion; sluggishness."[20]

God has prearranged a wonderful life for each of us, and we can make choices according to His will in order to enjoy it. I often say that anyone who merely lives according to the way he feels may as well stamp "destroyed" across his life.

Jesus is our model, and He was far from passive. He actively sought and lived out the will of God and resisted any temptation or pressure to do otherwise. The descriptive words we attribute to God even reveal Him as active—He saves, He redeems, He heals, He provides, He helps.

Jesus took time out to rest and pray, but even this was a willful decision. He knew He needed to do both in order to fully accomplish God's will. Many people today are sick due to stress, and they make one excuse after another about why they don't rest, but no matter how many excuses we make for wrong choices, the result is still the same.

Some people are too much like Martha, who was hyperactive and appeared to value work more than she should have. Mary, on the other hand, knew when to lay her work aside and spend time with Jesus (see Luke 10:38–42). We need to live well-balanced lives, and that comes from taking an active role in your spiritual life as well as your natural life.

As we spend time with God in fellowship, prayer, and Bible study, we will learn how to live properly. It helps us grow spiritually, and that is very important. Many Christians haven't made any spiritual progress since they were saved. They have a long list of bad habits they intend to give up, but they are not actively doing anything that will help them do so. Don't sit idly by and allow life to happen to you. Choose to live life "on purpose."

> *Don't sit idly by and allow life to happen to you. Choose to live life "on purpose."*

> *So much attention is paid to the aggressive sins, such as violence and cruelty and greed with all their tragic effects, that too little attention is paid to the passive sins, such as apathy and laziness, which in the long run can have a more devastating and destructive effect upon society than the others.*
>
> Eleanor Roosevelt[21]

Non-activity can be as devastating as evil activity. Dietrich Bonhoeffer said, "Silence in the face of evil is itself evil: God will not hold us guiltless."[22] In a world where there is so much to be done, how can we live a day without finding something to do that matters?

Go for It!

Why not make a decision that you are going to pursue the best life you can possibly have, and then actively go for it! Just wanting a good life won't produce one. We have to do what it takes to get what we want. Every effect has a cause behind it! We are encouraged frequently in the Bible to be alert, active, and consciously aware of what is happening around us.

These scriptures make it clear:

> And what I say to you I say to everybody: Watch (give strict attention, be cautious, active and alert)!
>
> Mark 13:37 (AMPC)

> Therefore then, since we are surrounded by so great a cloud of witnesses [who have borne testimony to the Truth], let us strip off and throw aside every encumbrance (unnecessary weight) and that sin which so readily (deftly and cleverly) clings to and entangles us, and let us run with patient endurance and steady and active persistence the appointed course of the race that is set before us.
>
> Hebrews 12:1 (AMPC)

Please notice the words in these scriptures that instruct us to be aggressively active in pursuing the kind of life Jesus died for us to have and enjoy. The writers of mark and Hebrews use words like *cautious, active, alert, strip off, throw aside, run, endure, be steady*, and *persistent*. Those are action words—words we can use in our lives as we seize each day.

I heard about a little boy who fell out of the bed in his sleep. His father picked him up and put him back in bed. He asked him, "Son, what happened?" The little boy responded, "I fell asleep too close to where I got in."

Many Christians today have fallen asleep too close to where

they got in. They are not in danger of falling out of salvation, but they have made no spiritual progress since they were saved. God expects us to make steady progress. Anything alive is always moving and changing; it is growing. If a pool of water is not moving, if fresh water is not flowing in and flowing out, it becomes stagnate and useless.

God's Word rebukes "sleepy Christians." They are told to wake up!

> *Therefore He says, Awake, O sleeper, and arise from the dead, and Christ shall shine (make day dawn) upon you and give you light.*
>
> Ephesians 5:14 (AMPC)

We are living in critical times. Danger and deception lurk all around us, but by remaining alert and active we will be safe. In his letter to the believers in Rome, Paul wrote that it was a critical hour and it was high time for them to "wake up" and rouse themselves to reality. He said that final deliverance was nearer than when they first believed (see Romans 13). Paul believed that Jesus was returning soon even in his day, so how much closer is that time now?

Surely, we want to be ready for Christ's return. We must not be like the five foolish virgins in Matthew 25 who fell asleep and were unprepared when the bridegroom returned.

Jesus told this story to illustrate an important lesson. He said there were ten virgins—five were wise and five were foolish. They all took their lamps (light) and went to wait for the bridegroom. Five were foolish because they had no forethought, but five were wise and they took with them extra oil just in case their journey was longer than expected. Passive, inactive, lazy people never do anything extra. They expend just enough energy to get through the day!

In the end of the story, the five foolish virgins were left behind because they were not prepared. When the bridegroom arrived, they tried to get prepared, but it was too late (see Matthew 25:1–12).

How many people wait until it is too late to do the right thing? They did not take action to do the right thing when they could have, and, although they now regret their choices, they have already lost something they cannot get back.

We can be fully aware of the good life God has provided for us in Jesus, and the good things He wants to do through us. Each day we can awake from our sleep and go for it!

When the apostle John was on the Island of Patmos, where he received from God the messages we now call the Book of Revelation, he was given seven letters for seven different churches, and many of them contained rebuke, correction, and warning as well as encouragement.

Jesus told the Church of Laodicea that they were neither hot nor cold and because of that He would spew them out of His mouth (see Revelation 3:15–16). I am not going to venture an opinion on exactly what that means, but at the very least it means they were distasteful to Him. They were complacent, lukewarm, and neither for Him nor against Him. His harsh words were actually spoken out of His great love for them, because He hoped they would wake up and become active.

To the church in Thyatira, He wrote that He knew their record of works, their love and faith, service and patient endurance, but that He had one thing against them (see Revelation 2:18–29). They tolerated Jezebel, who was actively leading others into sin! In other words, they were inactive against sin in their midst. Was it harsh for God to be unhappy with a church that was behaving so well in so many ways and that had only one problem? No, it was not harsh at all. God expects us always to be progressing, and that requires the confrontation of evil wherever we find it.

We cannot change all the evil people in the world, but we can make sure that we are not comfortably resting in their midst. Does being a successful Christian sound like a full-time job? It is! It is much more than a trip to church on Sunday that lasts forty-five minutes to an hour and a half, depending on what denomination you attend. If you attend a church, I encourage you to be actively involved in some way. If this is not possible at your church, then get involved in something that is increasing the kingdom of God.

In many instances, we have replaced service with sitting through a service. We are like the farmer who has replaced farming with watching programs about farming. Our fences are down, the weeds have choked out our harvest, and the enemy is running amok.

To the church in Sardis, He wrote, "I know your record and what you are doing; you are supposed to be alive, but [in reality] you are dead. Rouse yourselves and keep awake, and strengthen and invigorate what remains and is on the point of dying" (Revelation 3:1–2 AMPC).

He told the church at Ephesus that they had left their first love (Him) (see Revelation 2:4). To Pergamum, He said that some of them were clinging to false teaching and leading others into deception (see Revelation 2:12–14).

It certainly sounds to me like if we don't keep moving in the right direction, we will drift in the wrong direction. For example, I find for myself that if I don't study scriptures on the power of words occasionally, I will once again start saying things that are destructive. If I study walking in love, I am more inclined to do it. If I study giving, I become more generous. These are all things

I am fully aware of, but if I don't keep growing in God's Word, I will go backward. Christianity is about an active relationship with Christ. Church was never meant to be a spectator sport; we can all be active in the journey of life! We each have a home run waiting for us, but we have to keep swinging the bat.

> *We each have a home run waiting for us, but we have to keep swinging the bat.*

What Is the Problem?

Christians love God, and we believe in Jesus, so what is the problem? Why isn't the body of Christ (all believers) having a more positive impact on the world? There are many reasons why passivity has crept into our society, and one of them is having wrong priorities. We live in such a fast-paced world that few think they have the time to devote to their spiritual lives. I read that most Christians spend more time each day brushing their teeth than they do on spiritual growth! We simply cannot do all the world invites us to do and often demands that we do. It is important that we take inventory of our lives and prune things off that are not bearing good fruit. Jesus actually said that He would prune those who did bear fruit until they were bearing the most excellent fruit.

We have lost our ability to focus on what is truly important; the things that often get our attention are the ones that scream the loudest. In many cases we are addicted to entertainment, and cannot imagine a life without some of it each day. At one time entertainment required us to be actively involved, but now we usually take a passive role and expect to be entertained.

Most people today habitually complain about first one thing and then another, while they do absolutely nothing to make it any better.

A lot of people don't even bother to vote in elections, yet they constantly complain about the government. We can blame the problems in our society on a lot of things, but in reality our problems are due to people not taking action to do what they should when they should do it. People are too busy doing things that in the end don't really matter, and it leaves no time for the things that do matter a great deal.

Be honest! If you're not putting time into your spiritual growth and other things that really matter, are there non-essential things that you could eliminate and make the time available to do so? I am sure the answer is yes. If it is, then do it!

Does all of this sound exhausting?

I read that John Wesley traveled 250,000 miles on horseback, averaging twenty miles a day for forty years; preached 4,000 sermons; produced 400 books; and knew ten languages. At eighty-three, he was annoyed that he could not write more than fifteen hours a day without hurting his eyes, and at eighty-six he was ashamed he could not preach more than twice a day. He complained in his diary that there was an increasing tendency to lie in bed until 5:30 in the morning.[23]

I thought I was working hard until I read this. I don't ride a horse; I fly in an airplane. I only know one language, and I cannot write fifteen hours a day without a lot of things hurting. We need more inspirational stories like this. I don't necessarily think we need to work as hard as John Wesley did, but we can let his example be a reminder to us to accomplish all we can with the one life we have.

We think the easier life we have today is the result of progress, and in some ways it is. But it seems that as we progress, we also regress in maintaining standards and values that were honored and admired for centuries. What has happened to quality craftsmanship? What about integrity? Honor? Duty? Family priorities? These and many other things have been relegated to a back burner in our lives, and the flame is about to go out. We can revive! We often pray for revival in the church, but how can we have revival unless we are revived? True revival comes from within. It is not an event that comes into town for a few weeks and then is gone again.

It is time for each of us to stir ourselves up, resist passivity and lethargy, and actively pursue God's will. You have a free will, and you use it all the time, so be sure you are using it to make the right decisions, ones that will produce what you say you want out of life.

Chapter Summary

- Passivity will keep you from enjoying the best life God has for you. In order to walk in God's plan for your life, it is important to take action steps.
- We learn how to live properly and are empowered to make right choices by active fellowship with God, talking to Him in prayer and Bible study.
- Why not make a decision that you are going to pursue the best life you can possibly have, and then actively go for it?
- In order to keep from drifting in the wrong direction, it is important to keep moving in the right direction.
- Instead of the "urgent," focus on the "important" things. Actively dedicate your time to the most important things in your life.

CHAPTER 16

Be Careful How You Live

Look carefully then how you walk! Live purposefully and
worthily and accurately, not as the unwise and witless, but
as wise (sensible, intelligent people).

Ephesians 5:15 (AMPC)

To be careful means to give watchful attention to, to supervise
and to be responsible for. Are you supervising yourself? If you
don't, you will make many foolish mistakes in life. In an effort to
help you be more careful about how you live, let me ask you some
questions:

What is your lifestyle, and would Jesus approve of it?

What are your habits, good and bad?

Do you have a purpose?

Are you living your life "on purpose" each day?

Do you have a plan?

Are you able to follow through with your plans?

How often do you fail to accomplish your daily goals?

Are you leaving a legacy?

What are you accomplishing in life?

These are not intended to sound like an interrogation, but are
offered simply to get you thinking.

To be careful really means to be wise, to choose to do now
what you will be happy with later. The Greek word that we now

translate as "be careful" was originally translated, "walk circumspectly." That word means to look all around, like one who is walking in a very dangerous place. This person as he walks is constantly observing where he should put his feet next. Each decision we make represents a step that we take in our walk with God, and we should make them very carefully, considering what the outcome may be.

Be an investor in life, not a gambler! Make right choices and be assured of eventually getting a right result—don't make wrong choices and gamble that you might get by with it. Most people who have a serious gambling habit may gamble and occasionally win, but in the end most of them lose everything.

As you read this book, if you are convicted of areas in your life where you know you need to make a change, I urge you not to put it off. Take action now, because if you don't, nothing will change!

We are building a life and we want to be cautious so that in the end, we will like living the life we have built. Our lives are built on the foundation of Jesus. There is no real life without Him, but after receiving Jesus, it is our choice how we build and the quality of what we use to build with.

> *According to the grace (the special endowment for my task) of God bestowed on me, like a skillful architect and master builder I laid [the] foundation, and now another [man] is building upon it. But let each [man] be careful how he builds upon it.*
>
> I Corinthians 3:10

Verse 12 mentions a variety of materials: gold, silver, precious stones, wood, hay, and straw. It is obvious what we should choose

to build with, but we don't always do so. Let us all ask ourselves
what kind of life we are building.

Are you building a life that you want your children to inherit?
Are you leaving a legacy to the world you can be proud of? As
we choose a lifestyle, we should realize that our children more
than likely will imitate what they see us do in many ways. We
need to be careful how we build, not only for ourselves, but also
for those we influence. Don't build your life with one of the more
inferior materials that are mentioned above, don't even choose
the middle-of-the road materials, but instead choose and prize
what is excellent and of real value.

There are other scripture verses that say the same thing as
I Corinthians 3:10, but in a little different way. Paul made it clear
in Ephesians that we are saved by grace not because of any works
that we have done or could ever do (see Ephesians 2:8–9). After
making that clear, he went on to say that God has planned a good
life for us and that we should walk in it. Please notice that we
have to walk in it, and walking takes effort, making decisions,
and activity.

> For we are God's [own] handiwork (His workmanship),
> recreated in Christ Jesus, [born anew] that we may do those
> good works which God predestined (planned beforehand)
> for us [taking paths which He prepared ahead of time],
> that we should walk in them [living the good life which He
> prearranged and made ready for us to live].
>
> Ephesians 2:10 (AMPC)

Since before the beginning of what we know as "time," God
has prepared or planned ahead for us to have a good life. The
prerequisite to the good life is to be born again by receiving Jesus

as our personal Savior through our faith. After that, God desires
that we go on to live the life He has made ready for us to live. He
has laid out good works that *"we may do them,"* and He has prepared paths that *"we should walk in them."*

We can clearly see that the will of God is for us to do good
things and live a good life. That is impossible without us having a
new nature, so He gives us His very
own nature through the new birth,
and then says to us, "Now you choose
this good plan and the good works
and walk them out in your life for my
glory." The message could not be any clearer: God provides, and
we choose!

> *The message could not be
> any clearer: God provides,
> and we choose!*

Be Careful Not to Be Deceived

How many lies do you believe? Deception means to believe a lie.
Most of us don't consider whether what we believe is actually true
or not, and the only way we can ever know is to compare what we
believe to God's Word. His Word alone is truth.

If you apply God's Word to your life, you will find that it works
exactly as He says it will. Don't merely take someone else's word
for it, find out for yourself! You cannot be strong in God on secondhand faith. Your mom may have a strong faith, or your grand-
mother, but you need your own experience with God. Many
people end up deceived if they believe everything they are told
without doing any research into the validity of what they are
being told.

In the beginning of my walk with God, I was taught some
things that simply did not prove to be correct. One of them was
that if I had a strong enough faith, I could avoid trouble and

tribulation. But as I studied for myself and developed my own relationship with God, I learned by God's Word and life's experiences that what I had been taught was not accurate. I spent a few years very frustrated because each time I had a problem I tried to have more faith, instead of using the faith I had to trust God and remain peaceful. I thought that if I had enough faith I wouldn't have the problem, but I was deceived, and the deception kept me in an area that prevented me from making any progress in my walk with God. Don't take someone else's word for what you should believe without studying the Bible for yourself!

As I started a journey to study God's Word myself and seek God for myself, I discovered that without faith it is impossible to please God, and that everything we do should be done in faith. We may have very strong faith and still experience trials and difficulty in life. God gives us faith to get through hardship victoriously. We are more than conquerors through Christ Who loves us (see Romans 8:37), but how can we be more than conquerors if we never have anything to conquer? Faith does not eliminate difficulty, but it does help us navigate it while trusting God to deliver us at the right time.

This is simply one example of how we can be deceived if we don't check things out for ourselves. Whether the teaching I heard was wrong or I was misunderstanding, it is still a mystery to me. But I do know that when we diligently seek God *personally* we will know the truth and it will make us free.

Do you have secondhand faith? The apostle Peter wrote that God's divine power has bestowed on us everything we need to escape from the rottenness and moral decay in the world, through the full *personal* knowledge of Him Who called us (see II Peter 1:3). We need *personal* knowledge! A passive, lazy person would be more inclined not to put out the effort needed to check things out for himself, but it is dangerous not to do so. A truly spiritual man examines things:

> But the spiritual man tries all things [he examines, investigates, inquires into, questions, and discerns all things], yet is himself to be put on trial and judged by no one [he can read the meaning of everything, but no one can properly discern or appraise or get an insight into him].
>
> I Corinthians 2:15 (AMPC)

I really like the Scripture I just quoted. It reminds me that the spiritually mature person does not swallow everything hook, line, and sinker. He examines, investigates, inquires into, questions, and discerns all things.

Deception is everywhere today. Many people actively do things due to deception that at one time would have been considered gross sin. God hasn't changed His mind about right and wrong, but society has changed its mind. We have to make sure we are not drifting downstream with the careless crowd, or traveling on the wide road that leads to destruction. We should carefully examine what we think, say, do, and believe, and make sure it is in agreement with God's Word. If anything in my life or yours doesn't agree with God, then we are wrong, not Him!

> God hasn't changed His mind about right and wrong, but society has changed its mind.

Jesus warned the people several times to be careful that they were not deceived and led into error. He mentioned that we would especially need to be careful the closer we get to the end times. No man knows the day or hour when Jesus will return, but we can discern the times if we pay attention.

In the last days there will be wars and rumors of war, nation rising against nation, and earthquakes and famines in many places. People will be afflicted and suffer tribulation for the sake of Christ, and Christians will be hated. False prophets will arise and deceive many, leading them into error. Many will be offended and the love of the great body will grow cold due to the lawlessness in the land (see Matthew 24:4–12).

You can go right down the list and put a checkmark next to the things Jesus tells us to watch for. They are all a reality today, so surely He is coming soon and we need to be careful how we live. We want to be ready and excited when He comes, and we also want to be a good example to those who are lost and need to make a decision for Christ before it is too late. You are important to the plan of God. You do have a purpose. Let your light shine, and make sure that the light God has placed in you does not become darkness (see Luke 11:35).

I just had a momentary flashback of several people I know who are trying to decide what *they* want to do with their lives! It made me feel sad for a moment. Is it really up to us, or should we be saying, as Jesus did, "Your will be done, and not mine!" (see Luke 22:42)? What if every Christian had the same attitude that Jesus had? That is exactly what God expects us to do. He wants us to discover His will and use our free will to choose His will. When we make the right choice, the Holy Spirit will energize us to follow through.

> Let this same attitude and purpose and [humble] mind be in you which was in Christ Jesus.
>
> Philippians 2:5 (AMPC)

Do we want God's will more than anything else? Are we serious enough? Are we living carefully? If not, we can make a U-turn and go in the right direction. That is what repentance is. It means to turn and go in the right direction. Anytime we make the right choice God will empower us to do the right thing.

Since deception is a sign of end times, what kind of deception should we watch for? Moral deception surely must be at the top of the list. A recent study from George Barna and David Barton has provided some astounding statistics regarding what American adults believe about specific behaviors that the Bible clearly states are sinful:[24]

69%   believe that divorce is acceptable for any reason.
67%   believe it is acceptable for an unmarried woman to give birth to a baby.
66%   believe a sexual relationship between an unmarried man and woman is acceptable.
64%   believe gambling is acceptable.
63%   enjoy sexual thoughts and fantasies about someone they are not married to.
63%   live with someone of the opposite sex without being married.
47%   have no problem using marijuana for recreational purposes.
44%   use profanity.
43%   look at pornography.
42%   have had an abortion.
34%   get drunk.
32%   of teenagers have sex.

Less than 3 percent claim that when they make a moral choice they strive to be consistent with biblical standards. Only 34 percent believe there is an absolute moral truth.

Looking at some of these statistics, I definitely believe that many people are deceived. I have chosen to order my life and conduct according to God's Word because it is the one thing that consistently produces good results in my life. I have lived life without God and I have lived life with Him, and I can promise you that "with God" is better!

There are people who choose not to believe that God exists or that the Bible is true, and that is, of course, their choice, but I sincerely believe they will ultimately be very sorry. I urge you to make the right choice, because our choices become our lives.

Things in the world look bleak now, but they can change if each of us will do our part. We are only responsible before God for our part, so if we do that, He will take care of us. Instead of complaining about the way things are in the world, let's ask God what we can do to change it and then follow His lead.

Things will be much worse in the future if something isn't done quickly, and we are the ones who need to do it. Each of us can make sure we are representing Christ properly and not compromising in order to fit into a society we don't even like. If each one of us begins to be more careful about how we live, it may take time, but things in our society can be turned around.

There are many wonderful Christians who love God and live by a firm moral standard. They are the lights that are still turned on, but we need more lights and we need them shining brightly! Let's all shine together!

Be Careful What You Hear

We have a responsibility to be careful about what we listen to. Just because someone wants to talk, that doesn't mean we should listen. Words have power and when they get in us, they can influence what we think if we are not cautious.

I've heard that only 25 percent of Christian students who enter college come out with their faith intact. Shocking! They sit in classes and are assigned books to read that undermine their Christian faith, and over a period of time what they are hearing can have an adverse effect on them unless they know how to resist what they know is not true.

Young Christians going into college should be well informed about what they are going to be confronted with. The devil has instigated an all-out attack to remove God from everything possible. Many of our key universities that were originally founded and led by great men and women of God are now totally secular in their approach to education. God has been taken out of our history books, and it is having a very negative impact on society. Life without God simply doesn't work! He is the creator of all life, the owner and manager of all things, and the sustainer and maintainer of the universe. So how can things possibly work without Him? (See Hebrews 1:3.)

If a young person enters college without being firmly grounded in his Christian faith, personally knowing Scripture, his mind will be confronted with many theories and ideas that are popular but not biblical. Evolution, for example, is still called a theory, and yet 75 percent of students believe in evolution rather than creationism. The professors appeal to the students' reasoning and tell them it is unreasonable to believe in God, but too much reasoning can easily deceive a person.

The spiritual man doesn't reason, he discerns, and there is a big difference. Something may sound right to my mind, and yet I might not have any peace about it in my spirit. If that is the case, I should always follow peace. The Amplified translation of the Bible says that the mind of the flesh is sense and reason without the Holy Spirit (Romans 8:6). When we live in the realm of sense and reason alone, we are bound to be deceived! Thankfully, we also have the mind of the Spirit, and it is life and life eternal. We have the mind of Christ (see I Corinthians 2:16). We have the ability to think as Christ does, and when we do it will surely protect us against deception.

Be Careful about Listening to Gossip

Don't listen to gossip. If the person you are listening to is talking about someone else to you, they will talk about you to someone else. The Bible warns us against gossip in many places. One good example is found in Proverbs. It says:

> Whoever goes about slandering reveals secrets; therefore do not associate with a simple babbler.
>
> Proverbs 20:19 (ESV)

The sad thing about gossip is that once we have heard a criticism about another person, even if we don't want to believe what we have heard, it often makes us more suspicious of him or her. We should protect ourselves from the poison of gossip by stopping gossipers the moment they get started. Unless they have a really good reason for telling you what they are about to tell you, you don't need to hear it.

Paul told Timothy to always shut his mind against stupid controversies over ignorant questions because they foster strife (see II Timothy 2:23). In other words, "Don't listen to it."

Be Careful Whom You Associate With

Don't associate "with him who talks too freely" (Proverbs 20:19 AMPC). Don't make friendships with those given to anger (see Proverbs 22:24). Don't associate with those given to change, because they are unstable and unreliable (see Proverbs 24:21). Don't associate closely and habitually with those who are: immoral, greedy, do not give God first place in their lives, foul-mouthed (slanderous, reviling, critical, negative), a drunkard, a swindler, or a robber (see I Corinthians 5:9–11).

With this many instructions about whom not to associate with, it must be really important. A man's friends say a lot about him. Light doesn't fellowship with darkness (see II Corinthians 6:14). This doesn't mean that we should or even can avoid all people with ungodly traits, but we would be wise not to choose them as close associates.

We do choose our friends, and it's important that we choose them wisely. Choose friends you can trust, you can admire and respect, and you would like to learn from. If we spend a lot of time with someone, we may adopt the mannerisms and habits of that person and not even be aware that we are doing it. People influence us, so it is essential that we guard our heart, for out of it flow the springs of life (see Proverbs 4:23).

Being careful requires that we put some thought into what the outcome of our actions will be, and then make choices that will produce what we desire. Being *careless* allows us to follow emotions and just do anything without considering what the results may be. God desires that we be *careful* how we live so we can enjoy the good plan He has prearranged for us.

Be Careful How You Behave

I therefore, the prisoner for the Lord, appeal to and beg you to walk (lead a life) worthy of the [divine] calling to which you

have been called [with behavior that is a credit to the sum-
mons to God's service].

Ephesians 4:1 (AMPC)

We are given several encouragements in God's Word to be careful how we behave. It is obvious that people see our behavior, and by that they form their opinions of us. As representatives of Christ, it is vital that our behavior is an outward display of what we say that we believe as Christians.

Tremendous damage has been done to the cause of Christ due to hypocritical behavior of some Christians throughout history. A hypocrite is someone who teaches others to do what he does not do himself.

People in the world watch those who claim to be Christians, and evil people are looking for an excuse to make an accusation against them. The apostle Paul urges us to live above reproach, so those in the outside world can find no fault with us (1 Timothy 3:2–7).

Christians are not perfect in their behavior. We do make mistakes, but we can still strive to do our best and always remember that we are God's representatives in the earth. Let's live more carefully, being watchful and cautious, and as we do, it will not only improve our own lives, but it will also be a good example to others.

Chapter Summary

- To be "careful" really means to be wise—to choose to do now what you will be happy with later.
- God has graciously planned a good life for you to live.

- If you apply God's Word to your life, you will find that it works exactly as He says it will.
- Faith does not eliminate difficulty, but it does help us navigate it while trusting God to deliver us at the right time.
- You are important to the plan of God. You do have a purpose.
- When you choose God's will, the Holy Spirit will energize you to live out that decision.

CHAPTER 17

What Are You Doing with What God Has Given You?

A man by his sin may waste himself, which is to waste that which on earth is most like God. This is man's greatest tragedy and God's heaviest grief.

A. W. Tozer

Waste of any kind is sad, and certainly the waste of an entire life is the saddest of all. What we do today is important because we are exchanging a day of our life for it. We all know people who we would say have wasted their lives, but we should remember that a life wasted happens one day at a time. To waste one's entire life one has to waste many things: time, talent, money, resources, energy, health, et cetera.

We are always spending something, and when we do, we are either wasting it or investing it. God doesn't want you to waste your life—He wants you to invest it and bear good fruit.

Jesus once fed five thousand men, in addition to women and children, with a boy's lunch that consisted of five loaves of bread and two fish. He performed one of the greatest miracles that we read about in the Bible. After the people had eaten and were full, Jesus said this:

Gather up now the fragments (the broken pieces that are left over), so that nothing may be lost and wasted.

John 6:12 (AMPC)

Many people would have considered the leftovers trash, but not Jesus. He made sure nothing was wasted. In much the same way, some people are considered by others to be trash, good for nothing, but not by Jesus. He actually chooses and uses those the world would treat with contempt and throw away (see I Corinthians 1:27–28). I was one of those who would have been rejected, so I am very glad that Jesus doesn't like waste. He can do a lot with broken pieces!

We can follow Jesus' example and be careful not to waste what He has given us.

In the Old Testament, we read of God's command to the farmers not to waste the fragments left on the edges of their fields after harvest, but to let the poor come in and glean them (see Deuteronomy 24:19).

Perhaps you feel you don't have much, but let's remember the very small lunch that the boy offered to Jesus. Jesus multiplied it and fed thousands of people. Instead of being so concerned about what you don't have, offer to Jesus what you do have and watch Him multiply it. If we think too little of what we have, we are likely to waste it, so remember that whatever you have, it is important! You are important!

> *Offer to Jesus what you do have and watch Him multiply it.*

Maximize Your Time

The Bible says there is a time to be born and a time to die (see Ecclesiastes 3:2). Birth and death are both very important events, but the most important thing is what happens in between. If you do research on any famous person in history, you will see his or her name followed by the year he or she was born and the year he or she died with a dash (–) in between. The same dash is used on tombstones. A simple dash is used to express a person's entire life! So much goes on in the dash, but the important thing is to examine what it is.

What are you doing with your dash?

Life often seems like a dash because time seems to go by quickly. That is all the more reason to make sure that our "dash" is filled with good choices that produce excellent results.

The apostle Paul urges us to make the very most of our time, not passing up any good opportunities. (See Ephesians 5:16.) Some opportunities are offered to us only once, and if we waste them, we never get them back.

When Esther was offered the opportunity to help bring deliverance to the Jews, she was afraid of being put to death in the process. When she seemed reticent to do what was being requested of her, Mordecai sent her this message:

> For if you keep silent at this time, relief and deliverance shall arise for the Jews from elsewhere, but you and your father's house will perish. And who knows but that you have come to the kingdom for such a time as this and for this very occasion?
>
> Esther 4:14 (AMPC)

The fear that Esther felt was understandable, but if we want to seize God's timing in our lives, we will need to be willing to do God's will even if we must "do it afraid." Anyone who plans to wait for a time when they have no fear or opposition will miss many opportunities in life. Mordecai suggested to Esther that this opportunity that was before her was perhaps her intended destiny. She was called for just this time in history. Thankfully, she did what was requested of her and in the process she became queen and was used by God to deliver an entire nation.

When we seize the opportunities that are in front of us, we realize God's reward that is attached to our obedience.

When God put the opportunity before Dave and me to go on television, one of the strong impressions that Dave received from God was, "If you don't take this opportunity, it will never pass you by again." Not all opportunities are like that, but for some reason this one was. Who knows, perhaps God was looking for someone to fill a certain position in His Kingdom plan when he called you or me, and, as with Esther, if we don't say yes, He will find someone else!

Whether the opportunities are small or large, when we are given chances to serve God, it is an honor. There are billions of people on the earth, and God can choose whomever He wants to. If He chooses you for anything, redeem the time and, as the apostle Paul said, "buy up each opportunity" (see Colossians 4:5 AMPC). We can buy an opportunity with time. We can spend our time and use it to invest in God's plan and then we reap His reward.

Even something as simple as taking time to study God's Word is an opportunity, and we can take advantage of it or we can miss it. It takes time to study, so we buy the opportunity with time, but in doing so we invest in our future. The time is ours, and we can invest it or waste it.

What about the opportunities we have to encourage someone or to witness about the love of God? How often do we miss those opportunities because we are in too big a hurry or we are not sensitive to need in front of us?

> Behave yourselves wisely [living prudently and with discretion] in your relations, with those of the outside world (the non-Christians), making the very most of the time and seizing (buying up) the opportunity.
>
> Colossians 4:5 (AMPC)

Showing patience, kindness, and love to those we encounter daily is a very important ministry, and one we don't want to take lightly. I think

> I think each person we meet is an opportunity of some kind.

each person we meet is an opportunity of some kind. Even if we merely exchange a smile, it may leave a lasting impression.

Recently, I was in a jewelry store and the man waiting on me noticed a ring I was wearing and complimented me on how attractive he thought it was. I commented that it was a gift and he seemed to be even more interested, so I told him the story behind the ring. I shared that at one time many years ago I had felt that I was supposed to give away the one ring I had at that time to someone else. It was a sacrifice for me, not because the ring was expensive but because it had sentimental value and was my only ring. I gave it away, and about three years later a woman I did not know handed us a package and simply said, "This is for Joyce," and walked off. The package contained a ring box with the ring I was now wearing. It was much more valuable and beautiful than the one I had given away. I then went on to say to the man, "That is the way God is: if you give to someone out of obedience and love for God, He always gives you back more than you gave. It is called sowing and reaping in the Bible."

The man thanked me three times before I left the store for sharing that story. He said he had asked God for a blessing that day and he had received it in hearing the story. Obviously, the story meant something more to him than what I was aware of, but I could have easily missed the opportunity had I not been willing to take the time to share with him.

Being a blessing to people always takes a little time, so be sure you redeem your time and buy up each opportunity that comes your way.

Maximize Your Finances

The best plan to follow concerning money is to give some, spend some, and save some. By keeping these areas balanced, we can ensure that we are using wisdom with the finances God has entrusted to us.

Americans waste more than most societies have. It is important that we respect what we have and not waste it. Do I ever waste money? Yes, at times I do. I buy a coffee from a coffee specialty shop and end up not liking it, so it is wasted. I am attracted to a pair of earrings that shine and sparkle, so I buy them and never end up wearing them because they don't really go with anything I have. I could share other examples, but I just wanted to confess my waste before I speak to you about yours. I am sure that we are all wasteful at times and it is probably not intentional, but some could be avoided with some forethought.

We can all learn to waste less and have more respect for what God has given us. One of the ways I am trying to do that is to be sure I use what I spend money on, and if I am not going to use it, then I give it away. I also practice thinking about purchases, especially larger ones, before taking action. For some reason, a lot of things that seem so attractive in the store don't look as good when we get them home. Emotional purchases very often end up being regretted later.

Proverbs speaks frequently about prudence, which is simply good management. So the "give, spend, and save" principle is prudence in action. God's Word strongly urges us to give to God the first portion of all of our increase. I personally believe in tithing, which is giving the first 10 percent of what we earn. I also don't believe we should stop there, but that we should be very generous in giving and, when we are, we will not lack.

> *For if you give, you will get! Your gift will return to you in full and overflowing measure, pressed down, shaken together to make room for more, and running over. Whatever measure you use to give—large or small—will be used to measure what is given back to you.*
>
> Luke 6:38 (TLB)

When we work hard, it is good for us to reap some reward, so it is prudent to spend some of what you earn on things you want to enjoy. You don't want to be self-centered, but always denying yourself is not a good policy, either, because if you do, you will end up being resentful and feeling that your labor never produces anything for you personally. The Bible teaches that we should not muzzle the ox when it is treading out the corn (see I Timothy 5:18). In other words, everyone (even animals) needs to enjoy part of the harvest from their labor.

It is also wise to save some of all that we earn. When we do, we will be prepared for any unexpected expense that comes up. We will be able to help others in their emergencies, and we will eliminate a lot of fear and worry about what we will do if certain things happen and we have no money.

The Bible tells a story of a wealthy man who had run out of room for his harvest, and as he pondered what to do, he decided to build bigger barns and store up more and more. He wasn't using what he had—he was admiring it (see Luke 12:15–20). His abundance made him feel secure, but he would have been much better off if he had used a portion of it to bless others and perhaps himself.

The Bible contains a strong message about the importance of being a good steward of what God gives us. If our resource is time, money, energy, or talent, we are taught to use it wisely. We can invest it in order to reap a harvest for God. If we don't use it, we are in danger of losing it! When we use what we have wisely, it always produces more, but if we do nothing in laziness or fear, we lose what we have (see Matthew 25:14–28).

Maximize Your Energy

I believe we all have a certain amount of energy assigned to us in life and we need to manage it wisely. I worked too hard in some of the earlier years of my life, and I ended up not having enough energy for a few years due to illness that resulted from not getting proper rest and sleep. We cannot circumvent the spiritual laws that God has placed in the earth that rule all of us. We have all heard "Waste not, want not," but do we ever think of applying that principle to our energy?

If I sleep well for a sufficient amount of time, I am more productive during the day. If we live balanced lives when we are in our twenties, thirties, forties, and fifties, we will still have sufficient energy when we are in our sixties, seventies, and eighties. Be prudent with your energy. Don't run until you are exhausted each day and have no reserves left at all. Running on empty isn't wise. It makes us grouchy and keeps us from enjoying our lives.

It is very difficult to get a young person to listen to a message like this, but God has instituted laws of rest, and if we abide by them we will be glad later.

In addition to rest, we can also use the energy we have wisely. Getting angry, for example, takes a lot of emotional energy, so why do it? It doesn't add anything to your life, but it does take a lot from you. Worry takes a lot of energy and it is a total waste. Trying to control people and make them do what we think they should do is exhausting and it never works, so we would also be wise to avoid that. To be honest, if we just pay attention to what exhausts us and start eliminating those things from our lives, we would have energy to spare.

Maximize Your Talent

We are all gifted in some way, and we can use those gifts to benefit God and other people. The gifts we have are placed in us for other people, for their good and their enjoyment. A great singer entertains us. Her gift causes her to work, but in exercising the gift she is fulfilled, and we are entertained and blessed.

> The gifts we have are placed in us for other people.

We can look at any gift, talent, or skill in the same way. What would we do if nobody had the skill to be builders, doctors, or dentists? What if nobody could play a musical instrument, or teach, or cook?

Don't waste your life by wasting your abilities. Find employment that uses your gifts and you will love your job. We are all fulfilled and satisfied when we are doing what God intended us to do. I work hard, but I am doing what I am intended to do and, therefore, it is not stressful. It is a joy and I find fulfillment in doing it.

We are stewards of all that God gives to us, and He asks us to be faithful. He always rewards us for a job well done! More than ever, be determined not to waste your resources. Pray and ask God to show you areas where you might use more prudence. I believe that God gives us more than enough of everything we need in life, and if we manage it well, we will not lack any good thing.

Chapter Summary

- What you do today is important because you are exchanging a day of your life for it.
- God doesn't want you to waste your life—He has so much more in store for you.
- Even if you have to "do it afraid," make the most of every opportunity God puts in front of you.
- Financial prudence will keep you from wasting the resources God has given you.
- Rest and energy are resources that are important for us to use wisely.
- The gifts in your life are best when they glorify God and encourage other people.

CHAPTER 18

Seeing the End from the Beginning

The successful man is the average man, focused.
Author Unknown

In 1952, a woman by the name of Florence Chadwick was the first female to attempt to swim the twenty-six treacherous miles between Catalina Island and the California coastline. As she began this historical journey, she was surrounded by small boats navigated by people who watched for sharks and were ready to help her if she became injured or overwhelmed by exhaustion.

For hours Florence steadily swam, but after about fifteen hours, a fog set in that hindered her visibility and dampened her spirits. Florence began to have serious doubts about whether she could make it. She told her mother, who was in one of the boats, that she didn't think she could make it. She swam for another hour but eventually gave up. As they pulled her out of the water, Florence found out that she had stopped swimming just one mile away from her destination, the California shoreline. Florence later explained that she quit because there was too much fog for her to see the coastline. She couldn't see her goal.

As sad as that is, this story has a happy ending. Florence got back in the water two months later, determined to try once again.

And this time the results were much different. Though the same thick fog set in, Florence didn't give up the second time around. She swam from Catalina Island to the shore of California in a straight path for twenty-six miles. When asked what was the difference this time around, she explained that while she swam, she kept an image of the shoreline in her mind. She never lost sight of the shore because she focused on that image of the coast in her mind, and this way, she reached her goal.[25]

Whether your goal is winning a gold medal for a sport you love or to lose twenty pounds, you will need to keep the goal in front of you, especially during those foggy times when you are tired and your journey seems long.

> *Let your eyes look right on [with fixed purpose], and let your*
> *gaze be straight before you.*
>
> Proverbs 4:25 (AMPC)

Like a well-crafted meal, an "on-purpose" life has many key ingredients: determination, time management, scheduling and planning, following through, and wisdom, just to name a few. All of these elements are important, but perhaps the ingredient that brings them all together is *focus*.

Focus is directed attention. It is having a goal, aiming for a target, and not being easily distracted. Focus is the determination to stay on target and not allow other things to distract you.

I read that golf great Ben Hogan had tremendous focus. The story is told that Hogan was standing over a crucial putt in a golf tournament when suddenly a loud train whistle blared in the distance.

Hogan didn't flinch. He sank the putt. Later, when Hogan was asked if the train whistle bothered him, he replied, "What whistle?"[26]

Ben Hogan had talent, but that may not have been his greatest asset. There are many talented people who do very little in life. We don't have to be especially talented or mentally brilliant in order to accomplish great things, but as the quote I shared at the beginning of this chapter says, "The successful man is the average man, focused!"

All too often, people who accomplish very little in life assume they are just not as talented or brilliant as other people, but if they studied and emulated the habits of those who do great things, they would observe that the ability to stay on target (focus) was the main discipline that made them great. Just a little bit of research into history reveals the fact that ordinary people do extraordinary things if they apply the proper guidelines to their lives.

Zig Ziglar said, "I don't care how much power, brilliance or energy you have, if you don't harness it and focus it on a specific target, and hold it there, you're never going to accomplish as much as your ability warrants."[27]

If we cannot stay focused, should we merely blame distractions? Ben Hogan didn't, and neither should we. He had developed an ability to live with fixed purpose.

Perhaps more than ever, we live in a society full of distractions. We cannot keep the whistles from blowing! In this digital age there is always a new screen to look at, a new tab to click, a new e-mail to read, and a new social network to update. These modern realities aren't bad things, but they can be distracting things. It is easy to get so preoccupied with little things that we forget the big picture. As beneficial as social media has become, it is also one of the biggest distractions in many people's lives. We should use it at our discretion and not let it control us!

Technology isn't the only distraction in our lives. Hectic

schedules, unhealthy comparisons, financial pressures, the opinions of others, and so many things can cause us to lose sight of what's important. But if we are going to accomplish the goals we have and enjoy our life in Christ, it is important that we learn the art of being focused.

With the help of the Holy Spirit, we can each find our path to focus. Dave can sit and read and never lose his focus with all kinds of commotion going on around him. He has tinnitus in both ears, which is ringing, or a high-pitched noise. He says it doesn't bother him at all because he doesn't focus on it. Our family often says, "Dad lives in his own little world." Actually, he has trained himself to focus on what he wants to focus on rather than all the distractions around him.

Not everyone can stay focused as easily as Dave can, but we can find our own path. We may need to take measures to be in quiet places or leave the technology in another room, but the Holy Spirit will guide us if we'll pay attention to Him.

Patience

Patience is a big part of successfully reaching every goal that is reached. Very few things happen as fast as we would like them to or as we expected that they would. When you take the first step toward reaching any goal, make up your mind that you are going to finish no matter how long it takes.

> Make up your mind that you are going to finish no matter how long it takes.

Having the right mind-set from the beginning is a key ingredient in reaching your goal. Keep in mind what you want to accomplish and avoid focusing on how long and difficult the journey is. When tempted to lose focus and get distracted, ask yourself how you are going to feel at the end of the day if you allow yourself to wander from thing to thing, instead of staying on target. Remember that personal satisfaction and fulfillment are some of the best feelings in the world. It simply makes us feel good to know that we managed ourselves well.

Even when you do get distracted for a period of time, keep going back to your original plan for the day. Don't allow yourself to feel guilty; guilt is a waste of time. Patiently begin again where you left off and keep it up until you reach your goal.

Steve Jobs said: "Focusing is about saying no."[28] We can all develop an ability to say no to many things in order to focus on one thing. When the apostle Paul said that his one aspiration was to let go of what was behind and press toward the things ahead, he meant, in part at least, that he knew what to say no to. He said no to guilt and to thoughts that kept him trapped in the past. He focused on the goal of winning the prize that God was offering Him in Christ (see Philippians 3:13–14).

Some of our spiritual goals are never completely reached in this lifetime, but we still patiently press toward them. I would love to never do anything wrong, and to love everyone perfectly, but I have not arrived and won't until I get to Heaven. But I am constrained by my love for God to keep pressing toward the goal.

Never Give Up!

I have often said the one thing I have done that has been the most helpful for me in reaching my goals is that I have not given up. It takes no special talent to give up, but it does take focus and determination to refuse to give up. Not giving up is especially difficult in the foundation-laying phase. Strong foundations are vital to the success of the remainder of what we hope to build in life.

When we plant a seed in the ground, we have given up our seed and see nothing for a long time that indicates that our sacrifice was worth it. But eventually something comes out of the ground, and it grows into a thing of beauty and amazement. It grows into something that many others can enjoy.

Instead of giving up when you don't see anything in the natural, remember how Florence Chadwick swam through the fog toward the shore. Make up your mind to keep swimming while keeping the coastline (your goal) in mind.

I have had a great many goals in my life. The idea of actually reaching most of them seemed quite impossible at the outset, but many of them are a reality in my life now. I am quite ordinary, but I "keep on keeping on" and have no plans to quit. Don't let being ordinary stop or hinder you from trying to do something great.

> *Don't let being ordinary stop or hinder you from trying to do something great.*

Remember that most of the men and women we read about in the Bible, those we call heroes of faith, were very ordinary. They were fishermen, tax collectors, ex-prostitutes, shepherds, maidens, and even a woman who had been demon-possessed! No one is exempt from being used by God. All it takes to succeed is faith in God and determination!

You will find your way if you keep going forward. We learn as we go. For example, I had to learn that I could not do everything I was excited about, but once I knew what to focus on, I was on my way to success.

Holding on to our dreams is difficult in the foundation-laying years, but if we are patient during that season, the building will last. Don't be discouraged if you have planted seed and you don't see a harvest yet. Just keep trusting God and doing good (Psalm 37:3) and soon you will see the evidence of your harvest.

Strong Roots

If we want to have good fruit, we must be patient enough to develop strong roots. I wasted a lot of time trying to build a ministry without first building myself spiritually. We need time to become rooted and grounded in Christ as we are instructed to do (see Colossians 2:7). Jesus must be the foundation of everything else in our lives. I think it is safe to say that the majority of people who fail in life, or who drift through life never really accomplishing anything, do so because they fail to put God first at all times. Putting God first means to study His Word, pray, fellowship with Him, learn what His will is, and pursue it with all of your might. Love God first and you will probably end up getting the rest of what you love! Christ must be the foundation of our lives. Taking time to build a strong relationship with Him will ensure that your life will be built on solid ground.

Unless we keep God first at all times, we will not have sufficient energy to accomplish what we intend to do, nor will we do it with peace and joy. There are people who do great things without leaning on God, but they are usually miserable in the process, and they make the people around them miserable, too. We are created by and for God and nothing really works right without Him.

I have discovered in my journey with God that we learn as we step out in faith and try things, not as we sit idly by and do nothing. I have met many people on my journey, and I have learned what to do from some of them and what not to do from others. Does that sound strange? If so, I understand, but let me explain.

Obviously, I do learn good things from people, but I have discovered that I can learn even more by watching the mistakes people make and not repeating them. For example, I have been on the receiving end of having a boss who mistreated his employees, so I learned not to do that. I have been with people who refuse ever to admit they are wrong and their behavior has been so disturbing that I learned not to do that. I have been with people who are prideful and talk of nothing but themselves and their ministries, and I decided not to do that. I could go on, but I hope you are seeing my point.

Pay attention to the things that people do that hurt you and make a conscious decision not to do them to others.

One Mistake We Never Want to Make

One other mistake I have seen others make that I never want to repeat happens when promising people with great opportunities in front of them give up. They gave up

> Don't make the mistake of letting your mistakes cause you to give up!

because the way was difficult, the journey slow, or they became weary, and some of them fell into sin and never recovered. It is a sad thing to watch and something I never want to do. Don't make the mistake of letting your mistakes cause you to give up!

You can recover from mistakes because God is forgiving and merciful, but you cannot recover if you quit. Believe me when I say that we all make mistakes, and plenty of them. God knew that we would mess up, and that is precisely why He sent Jesus to forgive us and the Holy Spirit to help us. But the Holy Spirit will never help you give up, because God has a plan and a purpose for your life. So no matter where you are on the track of life, keep running your race. Keep the finish line in mind and stay focused on it.

Do you not know that in a race all the runners compete, but
[only] one receives the prize? So run [your race] that you
may lay hold [of the prize] and make it yours.

I Corinthians 9:24 (AMPC)

Chapter Summary

- In order to seize the day, make goals and go after them with all your heart.
- Ordinary people can do extraordinary things if they apply the proper guidelines to their lives.
- If we are going to accomplish the goals we have and enjoy our life in Christ, it is important that we learn the art of being focused.
- If you fail, patiently begin again where you left off and keep it up until you reach your goal.
- No one is exempt from being used by God. All it takes to succeed is faith in God and determination.
- We learn as we go, not as we sit idly by and do nothing.

CHAPTER 19

Finding Strength for the Journey

God is our refuge and strength, a very present help in trouble.

Psalm 46:1 (KJV)

Many find that they have the desire to do a thing, but no strength for the journey. God is our strength, so if we are trying to make the journey without putting Him first, we will fail. Our own strength will fail. Even youths and strong men have their limits (see Isaiah 40:30), but with God we are unlimited as long as we stay focused on His goals for us instead of our own. We cannot do anything *we want* to do, but we can do anything *He wants* us to do!

Even when we are pursuing something that is God's will, we still need to lean and rely on Him and trust Him to be our strength each step of the way. The single biggest mistake we are likely to make is to try to "do it ourselves." We are warned in Scripture of the dangers of leaning on frail man, and that includes others and ourselves. The prophet Jeremiah said it well:

> *Thus says the Lord: Cursed [with great evil] is the strong man who trusts in and relies on frail man, making weak [human] flesh his arm, and whose mind and heart turn aside from the Lord.*

Jeremiah 17:5 (AMPC)

Knowing what to do, or even how to do it, doesn't mean that we have the strength to take a task all the way through to the finish. We can go on willpower alone for a short distance, but all self-determination eventually fizzles out without God helping us! Discipline and self-control are both good and they are necessary, but where do we get the strength to exercise them? We know we shouldn't give up, but where do we get the strength to go the distance in a race that is much longer than we thought it would be? We get it from God Who is the source of all strength.

When Jesus said, "Apart from Me you can do nothing" (John 15:5), He actually meant exactly what He said. Jesus invites the weary to come to Him and find rest from their labor (see Matthew 11:28). We may work without Jesus, but we will labor and be weary.

Receiving Grace

We are saved by grace, and we can also learn to live by grace! Each day we need Jesus and His amazing gift of grace, just as much as we did the day we were born again. We need His undeserved and unmerited favor, His help, and His power to do what we need to do in life. We cannot earn or deserve grace because it is a free gift, but we do need to receive it through faith. I can offer someone in need twenty dollars, but that does not guarantee he will receive my gift.

I like to think of grace as the power that saved me from sin and the power that enables me to live the life that God wants me to live. For example, God wants me to be loving, patient, and kind, but I need His grace (power) to do it. God wants me to endure whatever comes with good temper, but I need His grace (power) in order to do it. God wants me to teach His Word, but I need His grace (power) to do it.

The apostle Paul spoke of a thorn in his flesh that he asked God to take away. Exactly what the thorn was, we don't know for sure, but we can discern that it harassed and was disturbing to Paul. Like most of us would do, Paul begged God to remove it. That is the easy answer—*"God, if you get rid of this, then I can behave the way I should!"* God told him that His grace was sufficient to enable him to bear the trouble (see II Corinthians 12:7–9). God didn't remove the difficulty, but He strengthened Paul in his weakness. Had God removed the thorn, that would have been a manifestation of His grace, but enabling Paul to bear the trouble was also a manifestation of God's grace.

Whether we need to be able to focus more, be more determined, or be more organized, we need God's grace (undeserved favor and power) to do it. If we need to change an attitude or a behavior, we cannot do it through struggle and fleshly effort; we need God's help and power to do it.

Ask!

The way to get help from God is to ask for it. You can wait until you need it to ask for it, or you can ask before the need arises, because you already know that without God's help, you will be unsuccessful in whatever you try to do.

When I go to the gym to work out, I don't wait until I am exhausted and feel that I cannot go on to ask for help. I ask on the way there! I already know that without Him, I won't even want to go, let alone do all I am supposed to do once I get there. I always want to treat people the way Jesus would, and I am quite sure that I will not unless God helps me, so I ask daily for the fruit of the Holy Spirit to flow through me and my personality.

God wants us to depend on Him in all things! He is the Vine

and we are the fruit-bearing branches (see John 15:5). Branches continually draw their life-giving strength from the vine. It is that life flowing through them that causes fruit to manifest on the branch. If there are stubborn dead leaves hanging on to the branch from last year, the new life that produces the new buds will push them off. In this way, you don't have to struggle to change

> You don't have to struggle to change yourself because you are changed by the grace (undeserved favor and power) of God.

yourself because you are changed by the grace (undeserved favor and power) of God. In order to bear good fruit in any area of life, just stay connected to the Vine (Jesus).

There are a few scriptures that I quote to myself or open the Bible to and read when I want to remind myself of the power in simply asking God to help me. They are James 4:2, John 16:24, Matthew 7:7–8, John 14:13–14, and John 15:7. I purposely am giving you only the reference to these scriptures to get you to do what this book is about—to personally take action.

Seize the information for yourself. When you do, it will mean much more to you than if I do the work involved for you. Lay the book aside, get a Bible, and look up these five scriptures and read them out loud. You will find yourself being much more inclined to ask God for help than you may have been before reading them. Harper Lee, an American novelist, said, "The book to read is not the one which thinks for you, but the one which makes you think. No book in the world equals the Bible for that."[29]

Things seem to mean more to us when we make a personal effort than they do if we only feed on someone else's work. I am thankful for computers and all the information that is available to me at the touch of a button, and I use them almost daily. But to be very honest, I am even more grateful for the years prior to computers when I had to dig and study, sometimes for hours, to learn what people today can get at their fingertips. Why? Because the effort I put into learning made what I know extremely valuable to me. One of the things that I thank God for on a regular basis is what I've learned, and it wasn't downloaded to my heart from a disk.

You can enhance your church experience tenfold by making notes of the Scripture verses your pastor or Bible teacher uses when sharing God's Word and then going home and looking them up and reading and meditating on them for yourself. In addition to studying God's Word personally, surround yourself with good resources that contain the Word of God taught by someone who is anointed by God to teach. Devotionals, books, and recorded messages are good resources. Even plaques displayed in your home that have Scripture verses on them are beneficial.

A friend of mine is very gifted and has a strong desire to minister to people, but she has experienced frustration at times because the right doors have not opened for her yet. I have felt led of the Lord to strongly encourage her to "serve the Lord with gladness," according to Psalm 100. When we serve Him with gladness, we can enjoy our time of waiting for Him to lead us into what we are to do next. I spoke with her recently, and when I asked how she was doing, she said, "I have painted on my office wall, 'Serve the Lord with Gladness!'" I have personally used many such reminders in my walk with God and found them to be very beneficial. Keep God's Word and your vision in front of you, and it will help you to keep pressing on.

Starting Your Day Right

One of the best ways to make the most of each day is to start your day with God! Form the habit of beginning to talk with Him before you even get out of bed. Thank Him for another day, and ask Him to help you live it for His pleasure. You can mention the things you know you need to do during the day and ask for His help in doing them well. If you have a meeting you are dreading, don't just grit your teeth and "try" to get through it, but ask for help in doing it with a good attitude. You can even ask God to help you enjoy it!

Every day is part of our journey with God, and we find strength for the journey by seeking Him early and consistently. There is nothing more vital to living an effective, intentional, "on-purpose" life than a daily time with God. This is a foundational biblical truth for any believer who wants to go beyond ordinary and live the extraordinary life Jesus died to give us.

> *There is nothing more vital to living an effective, intentional, "on-purpose" life than a daily time with God.*

The Bible teaches us that God is the Source of all things (see I Corinthians 8:6). Because God is our Source, daily time spent with Him is more than a devout obligation—it is a divine opportunity! It is our opportunity to be strengthened, encouraged, healed, equipped, and empowered for the day ahead.

You might look at time with God like charging your battery. My husband has an electric golf cart that he drives to the golf course that is close to our home. When he comes home with it, he always plugs it in so it is charged up the next time he wants to go. On occasion, if one of our children has borrowed it to take their children for a ride in the subdivision and failed to plug it in when they returned, Dave has been disappointed and not real happy when he went to use it and there was no power.

If we fail to plug in to God by spending time with Him, we will be disappointed and unhappy when we find that we need power and we have none. Take a branch off of a vine and watch it for a few days as an experiment. Each day it looks a bit more lifeless and in only a few days it is dead! That is the way we are, too. Off the Vine (Jesus), it doesn't take us long to lose our vitality, energy, zeal, enthusiasm, passion, determination, and joy. He is our Source!

In much the same way that a river is only as strong as its source, you and I are only as strong as our connection to God. When we purpose to spend time with Him by studying His Word and talking with Him, thanking and worshipping Him, we are filled with wisdom, strength, and courage for whatever is ahead, no matter how challenging it may be.

David spent time worshipping God (see Psalm 5:7). Mary sat at the feet of Jesus (see Luke 10:39). Moses went up the mountain to meet with God (see Exodus 19:3). Even Jesus took time to get away from the crowds and pray (see Mark 1:35). If "time with God" was important to them, it certainly should be important to us.

Hudson Taylor said, "Do not have your concert first and tune your instruments afterwards. Begin the day with the Word of God and prayer, and get first of all into harmony with Him."[30]

Many families sound like a band where all play a different song and none of their instruments have been tuned. They start bickering with one another from the moment they get out of bed. Things could have been very different if they had spent time with God first!

Yes, it takes time to be properly prepared to face another day, but many of us feel that we just can't find the time. After all, we are already too busy.

You will never find time for anything. If you want time, you must make it.

(Charles Buxton, English philanthropist, writer, and member of Parliament)[31]

Why is it so important for us to study God's Word regularly? It is more important than getting a college education. How can we know the will of God unless we study His Word? We cannot and never will. Perhaps some people don't study because they feel their lifestyle may be confronted by what they read. I will admit that as I study God's Word I am often reproved by it. It corrects me and helps me stay in what I call the "safety zone" of life. I do not in any way dread the corrections, but instead I am very thankful for them. God's Word helps me. It has power in it that enables me to do what I should, and power that enables me not to do what I shouldn't.

Any time you spend with God will actually save you time later. Martin Luther famously said that he had gotten so busy, he now had to spend three hours each morning in prayer in order to have the wisdom and strength to handle the rest of his day. No wonder he impacted the church forever with his revelation that we are saved by grace and not by works. He obviously worked hard, but only after having received sufficient power for the day through his time with God.

> *Any time you spend with God will actually save you time later.*

Just imagine what a different world we would live in if everyone on the planet spent time with God each morning in Bible study and prayer. All of the miseries from selfishness, crime, violence, injustice, oppression, slavery, and war come from despising or neglecting the precepts contained in the Bible, but if people studied them daily, the world would be a different place.

We cannot make other people's decisions for them, but we can decide for ourselves. I have made my decision, and I see the result in my life. God is my strength and a present help in trouble. He is my enabler. Each day is a gift, and I choose to seize it and do the most I can with it. I urge you to do the same.

Chapter Summary

- God will always give you the strength to do the things He calls you to do and live the life He's purposed for you to live.
- Grace is both the power that saves us from sin and the power that enables us to live the life that God wants us to live.
- The way to get help from God is simply to ask Him.
- In order to bear good fruit in any area of life, just stay connected to the Vine (Jesus).
- The best thing you can do to make the most of each day is to start that day with God.

CHAPTER 20

Seize Your Thoughts

[Inasmuch as we] refute arguments and theories and reasonings and every proud and lofty thing that sets itself up against the [true] knowledge of God; and we lead every thought and purpose away captive into the obedience of Christ (the Messiah, the Anointed One).

II Corinthians 10:5 (AMPC)

We are directed by the Word of God to take control of our thoughts. We are to learn God's Word and then seize any thought we have that doesn't agree with it. According to the apostle Paul, we lead our thoughts and purposes captive to the obedience of Jesus Christ. We are to "cast down" wrong thoughts, theories, reasonings, and imaginations. The Bible teaches us to *cast* our care on God, *cast* out demons, and *cast* down wrong thoughts. This is a violent word that means to pitch or throw. It reminds me of the word *seize*, which is also an active, aggressive word.

Aggression is required in order to seize or take control of our thoughts. It is easy to sit idly by and meditate on whatever happens to fall into our minds, but it is not the will of God. He wants us to use our free will to choose to cast down any thoughts that are not in agreement with His will.

Some thoughts are good, positive, energizing, loving, and beneficial, but not all of them are. The mind is actually a battlefield on which we do warfare with the devil. We are instructed to pull down strongholds that exist in the mind. A stronghold is an area in which the enemy entrenches himself and hides, hoping to be undetected so he can bring destruction. Satan works relentlessly to inject evil, sinful, and poisonous thoughts into our minds. His hope is that he will go unnoticed and that we will passively accept the thoughts as ours and then meditate on them until they become a reality in our lives. But the good news is that we have weapons that we can use to defeat Satan.

> *For the weapons of our warfare are not physical [weapons of flesh and blood], but they are mighty before God for the overthrow and destruction of strongholds.*
>
> *[Inasmuch as we] refute arguments and theories and reasonings and every proud and lofty thing that sets itself up against the [true] knowledge of God; and we lead every thought and purpose away captive into the obedience of Christ (the Messiah, the Anointed One).*
>
> II Corinthians 10:4–5 (AMPC)

By studying verses 4 and 5 together, we can readily see that we are in a war; we have weapons that will destroy strongholds when used properly. Using these weapons, we are to cast down all wrong thoughts. Our weapon is the Word of God, and it can be used in a variety of ways. We can compare our thoughts to the Word and when those thoughts don't agree, we make an adjustment and come into agreement with God. We can *meditate* on the Word, which helps to renew our minds and think good and beneficial things. We can also *confess* the Word out loud, and it helps us by interrupting any wrong thought pattern we are experiencing. We may also *pray* the Word! We can fill our prayers with Scriptures, putting God in remembrance of His promises as He has instructed us to do (see Isaiah 43:26). We may also *hear* the Word of God or *read* it, and it will keep our minds renewed to God's plan for our lives.

The Word of God is referred to as "the Sword of the Spirit" in the Bible (see Ephesians 6). Swords are used in battle, and they should always be sharp and close at hand for use. I urge you to remember that God's Word is a weapon for you to use against Satan.

A young man shared with us that his mother had died when he was fourteen years old and he became bitter and very angry with God. A few years later, he began to drink heavily as a way to dull his painful life, and he eventually became an alcoholic. One night, while on his way home from the bar, he hit a child with his car and she was killed. He was convicted of and imprisoned for manslaughter. While in prison, he returned from lunch one day and found that my book *Battlefield of the Mind* had been delivered to his cell by our prison ministry outreach. This is a book that teaches how important God's Word is and the part it plays in renewing the mind and teaching us to think right. We have been given the mind of Christ. We do hold the thoughts, intents, and purposes of His heart! In other words, we can think as God does.

As he read the book, he said that he realized his thinking was wrong and he began trying to adjust it. After serving his sentence, he was released from prison and shortly after that he attended his first Joyce Meyer Ministries conference, where he surrendered his life to Jesus. He now volunteers at our conferences anytime we are close to where he lives.

As tragic as it was, it was not the death of his mother that destroyed his life, but it was the way he thought about it. The devil can and does put evil and life-destroying thoughts into our minds, and if we don't know the truth (God's Word), we have no option but to believe him. The devil was delighted to tell the boy that it was God's fault his mother was dead and convince him to turn away from God in anger. He was even more delighted when he tempted the young man to be excessive with alcohol and eventually to take a life while he was drinking. He was very happy to see him in prison, but he was not happy when the book showed up and the man read it and found that he had another option to consider.

This young man learned that a battle was raging in his mind and that he could "cast down" or "seize" the wrong thoughts and replace them with good ones.

Do Your Own Thinking

The Bible instructs us several times to be watchful or to watch and pray. One of the things we should watch carefully is our thinking. If it is not in agreement with God's thoughts (His Word), then we should seize the wrong thought. We cannot seize the day unless we are willing to seize our thoughts regularly. A man becomes as he thinks (see Proverbs 23:7), or, as I frequently say, "Where the mind goes, the man follows."

You can do your own thinking. You can choose your own thoughts and should do so carefully. You can choose to think about a thing or not to think about it. All thoughts are seeds that we sow, and they will bring a harvest in our life. All seed bears fruit after its own kind, so don't sow what you don't want a crop of.

If we sow a tomato seed, we expect to get a tomato, but if we sow thoughts of hatred and anger, we often expect to have a great and joyful life. That will never happen! Sowing thoughts of anger and hatred will produce a bitter, miserable life. The world is filled with people who have miserable lives, but they often merely blame their circumstances on others instead of searching their own heart to discover what the true roots of their problems are.

As one who lacked knowledge, I did this same thing for the first third of my life. I thought according to my circumstances instead of thinking according to God's Word. The "thought seeds" I sowed continually produced more of what I hated. I was in a trap and could find no way out until I learned that if I wanted my life to improve, my thoughts had to improve first. Jesus invites us to believe—to believe His Word more than the word of any other—and when we do, things change for the better.

Renewing the mind and learning to think properly takes time and help from God, and He is always ready to help us do His will. God will help you—ask Him! The King James Bible uses the phrase, "gird up the loins of your mind" (see I Peter 1:13). The apostle Peter is telling us not to let our thoughts run wild, but to harness and control them.

If you want to make better use of your time, you will first need to make better use of your thoughts. Choose to be mentally assertive and proactive. Think about what you're thinking about, and if it isn't good or right, then think something else.

If you wake up in the morning and your first thoughts are, *I regret that I didn't stay focused yesterday and get more done. I just don't seem to have any self-control*, the moment you recognize that the thoughts are not in agreement with God's Word, you can choose to think, *I am going to let go of what is behind, and today is going to be a better day. God has given me the fruit of self-control, and I am learning how to use it.*

If our thoughts do not agree with God's Word, then they are either from the devil or the result of bad habits we have formed over years of not disciplining our mind. Either way, they are poisoning our lives, and we are the ones who must do something about it. God will always show us the right thing to do. He will even give us the grace (ability) to do it, but He won't do it for us! He has given us a free will, and we must use it.

Once you are well educated in God's Word (His thoughts), it functions like a light in your life that helps you quickly to recognize darkness. In other words, the Word of God that you have learned helps you recognize the lies of the devil.

Let me stress that this process takes time, and you will grow little by little. Don't give up on learning how to think right, because your life can never be right if your thoughts are all wrong. You won't reach a point where you never need to make an effort to think right! I have to make that effort daily, and so does every other person on the planet who truly wants to have the good life that God has made available through Jesus Christ.

From the Mind to the Mouth

Where do words come from? They are formulated in our thoughts, and they are powerful. God's Word teaches that out of the heart the mouth speaks (see Matthew 12:34). Our words contain the power of life and death (see Proverbs 18:21). We get a result from the words we speak, and we are encouraged in Scripture not to speak idle ones. If we seize (control) our thoughts, we are on our way to being able to seize (control) our words.

Have you ever thought, *I wish I hadn't said that*, after being rude or offending someone? I know I have. But wishing won't change a thing. The way to not blurt out words that wound, offend, and cause trouble is to change our thinking. What we think in private, we often speak in public!

> *What we think in private, we often speak in public!*

The psalmist David talked a lot about his thoughts and words. He meditated on God's Word a great deal, and he said that the

Word he had laid up in his heart kept him from sin. It was a light to him that gave him direction for his life (see Psalm 119:105). He also said that he had purposed (decided) that his mouth would not transgress (Psalm 17:3). This is one of my favorites:

> I said, I will take heed and guard my ways, that I may sin
> not with my tongue; I will muzzle my mouth as with a bridle
> while the wicked are before me.
>
> Psalm 39:1 (AMPC)

Notice that he *guarded* his ways and *muzzled* his mouth. Both of these words are action words; it sounds to me as if David was seizing the day! He made decisions about how he was going to live. He didn't merely wait to see what would happen and just drift along with it.

When Can I Just Relax?

We think all the time, so it's important to be careful all the time. However, the more you practice right thinking, the more natural it becomes. You will grow to a place where thoughts that don't agree with God's Word will actually make you uncomfortable. You will feel uneasy in your spirit. That is the Holy Spirit gently showing you that something is wrong, and when you pay attention to Him, He will reveal to you what it is. This may occur without you even being acutely aware that God is guiding you, but it is something that He promises to do.

You can depend on God to make you aware of wrong thoughts and to help you think His thoughts. He never asks us to do anything unless He is willing to help us do it. He knows much better than we do just how incapable we are of doing anything right without Him.

After all the things we have been discussing in this book about how active and alert we need to be, you may be thinking, *This sounds like a lot of work,* and you may be wondering, *When can I just relax?* Although controlling our thoughts does require effort and diligence, I can promise you that my life was much more tense and stressful when I was filled with negative and evil thoughts than it is now that I am actively and aggressively seizing my thoughts so they will be in agreement with God's will. Disciplining ourselves to stay in God's will is not hard, oppressive, or stressful. It is fighting God's will that gives us stress and frustration. Whatever diligence is required for us to remain in the will of God, it is easier than living out of His will.

We will make mistakes, and at times we may realize we have wasted an entire day thinking things that were ungodly, but God is very patient and will never give up on us. Jesus invites us to come to Him for rest and relaxation (see Matthew 11:28–29). We can stay in rest even when we make mistakes. We don't expect our babies to grow up overnight, and we are willing to help them when they fall. Our heavenly Father is the same way with us. He is merciful and kind. Just knowing that we want His will is enough for Him to keep working with us for as long as it takes.

> God is very patient and will never give up on us.

Power Thoughts

Power thoughts are thoughts that you can think on purpose that will actually release the energy you need to do a thing. Here are ten thoughts you can think on purpose that will help you seize the day:

1. God has given me this day. It is a gift and I will not waste it.
2. I can do all things through Christ because He is my Strength.

3. I am an organized person.

4. I trust God to guide me and help me as I walk through this day.

5. I choose to walk in God's will for my life.

6. I don't waste my time.

7. I plan wisely and I follow through.

8. I am an "on-purpose" person.

9. I will not waste the resources God has given me.

10. God loves me and He is with me all the time.

There are thousands upon thousands of other power thoughts. They are thoughts based on God's Word, and they will release peace and joy in your life. Do some "on-purpose" thinking early each day and it will help you get the right mind-set for the day ahead.

Chapter Summary

- When we meditate on the Word of God, it helps renew our minds so we can think good and beneficial things.
- We cannot seize the day unless we are willing to seize and take captive any thought that is contrary to God's Word.
- Renewing the mind and learning to think properly take time and help from God. He is always willing to help you—just ask Him.
- In order to make better use of your time, make better use of your thoughts.
- God will always show us the right thing to do. He will even give us the grace (ability) to do it, but He won't do it for us.
- The more you practice right thinking, the more natural it becomes.

Five Things to Do on Purpose

Therefore put on God's complete armor, that you may be able to resist and stand your ground on the evil day [of danger], and, having done all [the crisis demands], to stand [firmly in your place].

Ephesians 6:13 (AMPC)

Living "on purpose" for a purpose is an exciting and rewarding way to live. The "on-purpose" life we want to live is one that is in accord with God's purpose for us and His Kingdom. Although Jesus has provided a wonderful life for us, we must realize that Satan relentlessly tries to steal it. For this reason we must not be passive and assume the good life will be ours without a fight. Satan is our enemy, and he works relentlessly to steal the life that Jesus died to give us. We will have victory only if we stand firmly against him and all of his ways.

We can choose to live "on purpose" rather than by emotion! In this chapter I want to look at just a few of the ways we can do things on purpose and how they can make such a huge difference in our lives.

We can make a daily decision to stand firmly in our God-ordained destiny and not allow the world, the devil, or the desires of the flesh to steal it from us. This requires using your free will to choose God's will in each situation you encounter in life.

Last evening, Dave and I had a mildly heated disagreement, and the end result was that I did not get my way. I wasn't happy about it, and the more I thought about it, the more I could feel anger settling into my soul. At that point I could not just do what I felt like doing because I knew if I did I would certainly not behave in a godly way. I had only two choices: (1) stay angry and make myself more miserable, or (2) forgive Dave and refuse to be in strife.

I wanted to do the right thing, the thing that would please God, and I certainly couldn't go with how I felt and accomplish that in this situation. I purposely decided not to follow my emotions, but to trust God and let the situation go. I asked God to help me, and I began thinking about scriptures about forgiving others when they hurt us (see Matthew 6:9–15) and those that talk about the responsibility of the children of God to avoid strife (see II Timothy 2:24).

You might say I talked myself off the ledge. I was about to jump right into a full-blown session of anger and bitterness, but instead, I purposely chose peace.

1. Be Peaceful on Purpose

God's Word tells us to "put on" our shoes of peace (see Ephesians 6:13–15). In other words, we are instructed to walk in peace. Jesus said that He has given us His peace and that we can stop allowing ourselves to be upset, disturbed, fearful, and intimidated (see John 14:27). If we consider these two Scripture verses and decide to believe them, then we must admit that we have peace available to us, but we may not understand that we can be peaceful on purpose.

For many years I was deceived and thought that if my circumstances didn't calm down I couldn't calm down. By thinking in this way I was literally giving the devil control over my behavior. If he set me up to get upset by arranging for circumstances that were unpleasant for me, then I had an anxious and frustrating day. We need to know what our "peace-stealers" are and watch out for them.

Have you ever said, "My kids know what buttons to push to get me upset"? Even more important is to realize that the devil knows what buttons to push to get us upset. We all have different triggers, and it is time that we recognize them in order to stand firm and take charge of our lives. This is how we start living the life we really want on purpose.

Peace won't just happen! We have the task of being makers and maintainers of peace (see Matthew 5:9). The peace of God is in us as His gift to us, and we can learn to access it and hold on to it in the storms of life. God told the Israelites to hold their peace and He would fight for them (see Exodus 14:14). They obviously could remain peaceful, otherwise God would not have instructed them to do so. I firmly believe that we are capable of much more than we believe we are.

> *We are capable of much more than we believe we are.*

We have spent far too long asking God to do things for us that in reality He has already done and is waiting for us to claim by faith. But, practically speaking, how do we do that?

I practice talking to myself in tense situations. When I feel my peace leaving and stress coming, I remind myself that I can hold my peace by trusting God to take care of the situation. If I remain peaceful, He will fight for me. I breathe and think before speaking, and sometimes I even have to get away from the situation in order to give me time to minister to myself. Yes, you can minister to yourself. Remind yourself of the promises of God and meditate on some of the Scripture verses you have learned about being peaceful in the difficult times of life.

I remember a time during income-tax season that was challenging for me. We always have to pay, so I asked our accountant if she had an estimate of what we would owe. When she told me, I felt panic rising in me because what we had set aside to pay for taxes was extremely short of the figure she gave me. I could not believe we had estimated that far off, and neither could she. I was feeling more upset by the minute and was trying to talk to myself at the same time. "Joyce, stay calm. You need to investigate before you panic." After some looking at bank accounts and checking deposits and withdrawals, sure enough I did find the money. I had put it into an interest-bearing account to wait until I needed it and had forgotten I put it there. Boy, was I glad to find that mistake!

My point is that when we get unpleasant news, or a bad report of any kind, our first natural response is to get upset, even though that will do nothing to help the situation. Resisting the devil at his onset is what the apostle Peter tells us to do (see 1 Peter 5:9). We can stop ourselves from getting more and more upset (see John 14:27) if we will make the effort to do so. Talk to yourself and remind yourself that God is faithful, and there is always an answer to every dilemma.

We cannot hear from God or be led by His Spirit when we are disquieted. Peace has been defined as a "quiet heart." We need to have calm souls in order to discern what He would have us do in difficulty. Don't keep repeating the same old pattern over and over, having a circumstance you don't like, getting upset, saying things you shouldn't say, doing things you shouldn't do, repenting, and then doing it all again. It is time for something new! It is time to be peaceful on purpose!

2. Purposely Remember Your
Value as a Child of God

God's Word teaches us to "put on" righteousness (see Ephesians 6:14). Sometimes we have an identity crisis and, although we are new creatures in Christ through the New Birth (salvation) and have been made right with God, we can let the devil steal the knowledge of our right standing and value with God. Identity theft is a big business today, and many of us purchase fraud or identity theft insurance so we are covered in case someone hacks into our personal information and steals our identity. It has never happened to me, but I have heard that when it does, it is a real nightmare.

I think it is safe to say that Christians who do not remember who they are in Christ, that God loves them unconditionally, that He views them as being right with Him, will live miserable lives even though they don't have to. Satan fights against us, but we have instruction from God on how to defeat him and remain the victor at all times. But it requires doing some things on purpose! One of those things is to put on righteousness. "Put on" is an action phrase. It requires us to do something.

Let me make it as simple as I can: when we sin, we are often tormented with guilt and condemnation. We may even believe that God is angry with us and that we have to do something to get back in favor with Him. That is not the truth, but it is what the devil wants us to believe. God's favor is a free gift, otherwise it wouldn't be favor. It is ours through faith. When we sin, we can repent and continue to believe that although we did something that wasn't right, we never for even a moment lost our right standing with God. We stay covered with righteousness and wear it like a robe!

We see the phrase "put on" several times in the Bible and I have come to understand that it simply means "Do this on purpose." Don't wait to feel like it or expect someone else to do for us what we should do ourselves. Rather than being passive, seize or take control of the situation, your thoughts and attitudes, and line them up with God's promises.

You are a beloved child of God, the apple of His eye, and He is with you at all times. Don't let the devil steal your true identity. Know who you are, hold your head up confidently, and enjoy the life that Jesus has provided for you. Do it on purpose!

> Know who you are, hold your head up confidently, and enjoy the life that Jesus has provided for you.

3. Love on Purpose

We are taught in God's Word to put on love above all that we put on (see Colossians 3:14). That literally means that the most important thing we can do is to walk in love. Love is not a feeling we wait to have, it is a decision we make about how we will treat people—all people! We don't get to treat people who are good to us one way and then mistreat the ones who are rude and unkind to us. Like God, we should be the same all the time no matter what is happening around us.

Yes, I know that is a tall order, but we will never do anything God asks us to do if we keep telling ourselves how hard it is to do it. We can choose to believe that God will enable us to do anything He asks us to do.

Walking in love will require being generous in forgiveness, because the truth is we live in a world filled with imperfection. People hurt us, they may treat us unjustly, or be unloving to us, but God has given us a simple solution to not allowing the poison of bitterness into our souls. Jesus told us not only to forgive our enemies, but to be kind and good to them!

> *But I say to you who are listening now to Me: [in order to heed, make it a practice to] love your enemies, treat well (do good to, act nobly toward) those who detest you and pursue you with hatred,*
>
> *Invoke blessings upon and pray for the happiness of those who curse you, implore God's blessing (favor) upon those who abuse you [who revile, reproach, disparage, and high-handedly misuse you].*
>
> Luke 6:27–28 (AMPC)

We are told to forgive not for the other person's benefit, but for our own. When we forgive, we do ourselves a kindness and a favor because we are set free from the torment of needing to hate someone and wasting our lives being vengeful. We look at forgiveness from the wrong point of view. We think, *They don't deserve my forgiveness after what they did to me, and I am going to get them back and make them pay.* But it simply doesn't work. Often, the people we are angry with are enjoying their lives and don't know or care that we are upset!

We obviously cannot do what Jesus is suggesting in these scriptures unless we make a decision and do it on purpose. We will never *feel* like blessing someone who has been unkind or has treated us unfairly. But the good news of this book is that we don't have to feel like doing what is right in order to do it. People who forgive are strong people!

> We don't have to feel like doing what is right in order to do it.

I once heard:

> *The first to apologize is the bravest.*
> *The first to forgive is the strongest.*
> *And the first to forget is the happiest.*

Learning this truth about forgiving on purpose was life-changing for me. Being sexually abused by my father and abandoned to the situation by my mother left me with many ill feelings that filled me with bitterness and unhappiness. If you are unhappy, look for the root of the problem, because the unhappiness won't go away until the root is dealt with. We usually believe our unhappiness is caused by someone (or something) else, but it is usually our own attitude toward others and our circumstances that are the real culprits.

Forgiving people may not change the way you feel about them right away, but praying for them and being kind to them when possible will set you free, and eventually your feelings will heal. Jesus is our healer, but our obedience is what releases the healing that He has provided through His death and resurrection. Jesus came to show us a new way to live! Our instruction from God's Word is to "put off the old man and put on the new man" (see Ephesians 4:22–24). That simply means that we need to make a decision to live the new life that Jesus has provided, for it is the only thing that will bring the peace and joy we all desire.

Jesus did not come to do everything for us while we sit by passively doing nothing. He came to show us what to do and to empower us to do it. You can forgive! If it were impossible, then God would not have instructed you to do it.

Love requires forgiveness, and it also requires many other behaviors that may need to be practiced on purpose. Love is patient, kind, humble, meek, not jealous or envious, always believes the best, and never gives up (see I Corinthians 13:4–8). Wow! I know I have to ask God for help daily in order to manifest this kind of good fruit in my life, and you will need His help also. I highly recommend spending time with God in fellowship and in studying His Word, because the closer you are to Him the more you will become like Him. Our love for God causes us to want to do everything that He asks us to do.

Love also gives. When love sees a need, it is compelled to do something. Love must be active in order to stay alive. It flows into us from God, and must flow out of us toward others. A stream must be moving in order not to stagnate, and we are the same way. Just knowing the right thing to do isn't good enough—we must do it!

4. Purpose to Pray about Everything

God's Word tells us to lift up the shield of faith and with it we can quench all the fiery darts of the enemy, and to cover everything with prayer (see Ephesians 6:16,18). As we go through life, we find that the devil is good at throwing spears and fiery darts. Our position is to remain in faith and pray about everything that threatens or troubles us. I love what Paul wrote to the Philippians:

> Do not fret or have any anxiety about anything, but in every circumstance and in everything, by prayer and petition (definite requests), with thanksgiving, continue to make your wants known to God.
>
> Philippians 4:6 (AMPC)

I meditate on this scripture often in life. We can learn to meet every crisis with faith that is released in prayer. Faith is a powerful force, but it does need to be released to be most effective. We can release it by praying and by saying! I pray for God to take care of the situation, and I say things that agree with what I have prayed. Prayer mixed with worry and a negative conversation doesn't bring an answer.

> Prayer mixed with worry and a negative conversation doesn't bring an answer.

5. Do What Is Right on Purpose

God's Word teaches us not to become weary in doing what is right and to be assured that we will reap a good reward in due time (see Galatians 6:9). If we are honest, we will admit that at times we do become weary, and may not feel like doing what is right any longer because we simply don't seem to be getting right results. But that is precisely when we need to do what is right on purpose even though we don't feel like doing it.

There are some things we may know we should do because they are the right thing, but we may never want to do them as far as our feelings are concerned. For example, God's Word states that "if anyone fails to provide for his relatives, and especially for those of his own family, he has disowned the faith [by failing to accompany it with fruits] and is worse than an unbeliever [who performs his obligation in these matters]" (I Timothy 5:8 AMPC).

I had to make a choice to obey this scripture regarding taking care of my father, mother, and an aunt when they were elderly and unable to care for themselves. Because my parents had abused me while I was growing up, I had no fond feelings for them, but I knew it was the right thing for me to do. My aunt had no children to help her, so responsibility also fell to me, and, once again, I knew it was right to provide for her. Providing for their care has required a sacrifice of time and money over the past fifteen years, and, although my parents are deceased, my aunt is still living and needs care.

I don't do this because I feel like it, because, to be honest, there are times when I don't, but I know it is the right thing to do and I do it. The greatest hindrance to spiritual maturity is walking according to our emotions instead of purposely choosing to do the right thing. Even though we may not want to do a thing, we can choose to do it just because we love God.

Perhaps you find yourself in a position where you need to forgive someone who has treated you badly, or maybe that person needs your help in some way but you are finding it very difficult to give it. I urge you to do it because of your love for God and because you are committed to doing what is right.

> And become useful and helpful and kind to one another, tenderhearted (compassionate, understanding, loving-hearted), forgiving one another [readily and freely], as God in Christ forgave you.
>
> Ephesians 4:32 (AMPC)

Learning to use your free will to choose God's will is very important, and I think it is safe to say that if a person is willing to do so, he or she will live an extremely enjoyable and fruitful life.

Perhaps some of your purposes have been out of order, but it's not too late to make a change. Today you can decide that from now on you want to please God more than you want anything else in life and that you are going to do so "on purpose." Being an "on-purpose" person starts with a decision. That decision needs to be followed up with a lot of prayer, leaning on God, and trusting Him to enable you to follow through. Let's join together and be the best we can be for Jesus!

As we purpose to do the will of God in these five areas as well as others, we will enjoy life more because we will have the joy of knowing we are living for a purpose. Nobody wants to wake up each day and feel that he or she has no purpose in life. We need purpose to motivate us. We need something to be enthusiastic about! I am excited about living to do the will of God. I find it challenging and energizing.

Chapter Summary

- Living "on purpose" for a purpose is an exciting and rewarding way to live.
- You can learn to access the peace of God and hold on to it in the storms of life.
- You are a beloved child of God, the apple of His eye, and He is with you at all times.
- The most important thing you can do is to walk in love.
- Jesus came to show us what to do and to empower us to do it.
- You can meet any crisis with the faith that is released in prayer.
- The greatest hindrance to spiritual maturity is walking according to our emotions instead of purposely choosing to do the right thing.

CHAPTER 22

Take Charge of Your Life

The difference between who you are, and who you want to be, is what you do!

Author Unknown

We can spend our lives wishing, but wishing won't change anything. I often say, "We don't need wishbone; we need backbone." Being successful at real life takes more than passive wishes. To succeed, we need God, His help, and the willingness to make right decisions and to work hard.

There are people whom the world would say are successful and yet they have no relationship with God. Are they truly successful? I don't think so, because most of them are not truly happy and they are often woefully lacking in the relationship department of life. They may have money and fame, but that doesn't comfort them in the dark and painful hours of life. Many so-called successful people take drugs or drink alcohol in excess in order to get through the day, and that is a tragedy, not a success. There are a few people, I suppose, who seem to be making it without God, but I wonder how they will feel when all of this life passes away and they need to give an account of their life. They may be living like there is no tomorrow, but tomorrow will come. Today's choices are tomorrow's future!

> Today's choices are tomorrow's future!

This is a good opportunity to look at your life and ask yourself some hard questions. Things like, "What am I living for?" "Who am I living for?" "Am I prepared to meet God?" "When I die will I leave a legacy to be proud of?" "Am I enjoying my life?" and many other such questions. If you don't get the answers you want, then you need to take charge of your life and start living "on purpose" for a purpose!

The Word of God teaches us how to live a blessed life. It says that we are to order our conduct and conversation according to God's revealed will.

> Blessed (happy, fortunate, to be envied) are the undefiled (the upright, truly sincere, and blameless) in the way [of the revealed will of God], who walk (order their conduct and conversation) in the law of the Lord (the whole of God's revealed will).
>
> Psalm 119:1 (AMPC)

A blessed life comes from following God and His ways. The apostle Matthew speaks of a narrow road and a wide road (see Matthew 7:13–14). He indicates that the wide road is easy to walk, but it leads to every kind of misery. On the wide road you will always have plenty of company, and you can do whatever you feel like doing with no concern for the future or other people, but the end result is destruction.

The narrow path is the one that leads to having a truly successful life, and Matthew says there are relatively few who find it. It is more difficult to travel and is often a lonely path. The person who is intending to follow God will make some decisions that won't be understood by everyone he knows, but he will also reap an abundant harvest of joy and fulfillment in life. At the end of his or her life here on earth he or she will hear God say, *Well done, good and faithful servant. Enter into the joy, the delight and blessedness of the Lord* (see Matthew 25:23).

What Do You Need to Take Charge Of?

We asked our staff to respond to the two following questions:

1. What do you need to take charge of in your life?
2. What are the things or circumstances that keep you from taking control of those areas?

Here are some of the responses we received:

1. Eating too many snacks. Eating too many sweets. They are everywhere I go and I like them too much. I procrastinate about taking control.
2. Confronting a mother who used to be extremely violent and abusive but is now attempting to control me with silence and rejection. The fear of rejection keeps me from taking charge in this situation. I love her, but I don't know how to have a healthy relationship with her without ripping open some very old wounds.
3. Several people said they needed to take charge of negative thoughts and feelings toward themselves or about their life.
4. Time management is a huge issue for many people.
5. Unhealthy and ungodly feelings and attitudes toward others.
6. Some said they needed to get their spending under control.
7. Taking care of my responsibilities.

8. One person said that the reason he doesn't take charge in areas he knows are wrong is that he keeps justifying his behavior. (I thought this was a very honest answer.)

9. Thoughts and words.

You may relate to some of these responses, or you may recognize different areas in your life that need your attention, but one thing is for sure: putting off taking action until tomorrow, or at another time in life, is not wise. The sooner you make a change, the sooner you will be living the life you truly want to live.

Tomorrow

Tomorrow might possibly be the most dangerous word I know because it often describes procrastination. Many people intend to do the right thing tomorrow, or they are going to deal with the problems in their life tomorrow. Why wait until tomorrow? It is the path of avoidance, but it is not God's will.

There is a very interesting account in the Bible about a plague of frogs that came on Egypt because of Pharaoh's disobedience. Frogs were absolutely everywhere. In people's houses, beds, and ovens. They could find no place of refuge because the frogs had taken over all of the houses.

Pharaoh called for Moses and said that he would obey God if He removed the frogs. Moses then asked him when he wanted him to pray and ask the Lord for deliverance from the frogs and Pharaoh said, "Tomorrow!" (see Exodus 8:1–10).

I find this story to be amazing. Who in their right mind would have such a situation and decide to spend one more night with the frogs before being free of them? It sounds foolish, but we all do it at times. If we let the frogs represent things in our life that we need to deal with or take care of and think about how we tend to put it off until another time, we can see that we are doing the same thing Pharaoh did. We keep our misery, our guilty conscience, our unsuccessful life, our frustration, and many other such things, but we could be free if we would immediately obey God.

Taking charge of your life means that you will choose to do the difficult thing because you are interested in having a good end result. Taking charge of your life may mean not buying what you see at the store that stirs you emotionally, instead using the money to pay off debt you already have so someday you can be debt free. It may mean that you make peace with someone who hurt you because you refuse to live your life angry and bitter. It may mean that you make better choices concerning what you eat because you want to feel better and enjoy better health.

The discipline of making the right choice no matter how one feels is the road to a successful life. Seizing the day is all about making the best choices possible each day of your life. What you have today is a result of choices made in the past, and what you have in the future will be the result of choices you make now!

> The discipline of making the right choice no matter how one feels is the road to a successful life.

The apostle Paul took charge of his life. He said, "Therefore I always exercise and discipline myself [mortifying my body, deadening my carnal affections, bodily appetites, and worldly desires, endeavoring in all respects] to have a clear (unshaken, blameless) conscience, void of offense toward God and toward men" (Acts 24:16 AMPC).

I am aware that this doesn't sound like much fun, but it does bring peace and joy. I think that we often give up peace and joy in order to keep doing what we feel like doing, but we should remember that the fun we think we are having is short lived and temporary. I urge you to make right decisions today! Don't spend one more night with the frogs.

Here is a very simple example, but one that is easily understandable. I recently gained four pounds and wanted to lose it before I kept gaining more and more. I restricted my eating and it took about four weeks, but I did lose the weight. It was a lot more fun to gain it than it was to lose it. When Paul said that he deadened his carnal affections, he was simply saying that he didn't do all that he felt like doing because he knew the outcome would not be enjoyable.

I enjoyed myself while I was gaining the weight, but I was really hungry while I was losing it. I remember how I felt the day I got on the scale to weigh after not weighing for three months. First, I dreaded seeing the numbers come up because I already knew I had gained weight. Not weighing for so long was my way of avoiding truth. I felt frustrated and aggravated when I saw I had gained weight. The morning I got on the scale and realized I had lost the weight I had gained, I felt joyful and peaceful. I also realize I will need to continue on in godly discipline if I want to keep the weight off. Some people have gained and lost one thousand pounds in their life, but if you are someone who needs to take better care of yourself, then it is time to make a decision and stick with it.

I realize I am talking about only four pounds and to those of you who may need to lose a lot of weight my example may sound silly, but the principle is the same no matter what we need to take charge of. Living without discipline may feel good to the flesh for a while, but eventually we have to pay the price for it, and then that doesn't feel good. No person will be able to make changes that will get his or her life back into balance and do so without feeling any discomfort.

As the old saying states, "We all have to pay the piper." Dictionary.com defines "to pay the piper" as to pay the consequences for self-indulgent behavior. If you stay up late at night watching television, in the morning you will have to pay the piper by being tired and not feeling like going to work.

At the end of each decision we make in life something is waiting for us. Will you find peace and joy at the end of the decisions you make today, or will it be frustration, regret, and perhaps guilt? The choice is yours and only you can make it!

It Doesn't Sound Like Much Fun

Living a life of discipline doesn't always sound like much fun initially. We are very prone to wanting immediate satisfaction, and living a life of discipline doesn't provide that. But it does provide the life that you truly want! In the depths of our heart we all want a life of purpose. We want to see good results from our efforts and the time we have invested, but it only happens as we do the right thing over and over and then wait for our investment to pay off.

When we make good choices, they may not always appear to be good immediately. We often have to add patience into the mix and trust God that right choices always produce a right result if we won't give up. Doing something right once or twice never brings the result we desire. We must be committed to a lifestyle of making right choices over and above all else. This is living on the narrow path that will lead to the life we desire.

Discipline doesn't seem joyful immediately, but it will produce the peace of right living in due time.

For the time being no discipline brings joy, but seems griev-ous and painful; but afterwards it yields a peaceable fruit of righteousness to those who have been trained by it [a harvest of fruit which consists in righteousness—in conformity to God's will in purpose, thought, and action, resulting in right living and right standing with God].

Hebrews 12:11 (AMPC)

Your choices are yours alone to make. The Holy Spirit will prompt us to make the right decision, but He will not force us. The Amplified Translation of the Bible Classic Edition uses the phrase "under obedience to the promptings of the Spirit" (see Romans 7:6 AMPC). It is clear that the choice is ours. If we make the right choice, God will give us His grace (power) to follow through and do the right things.

It feels really good to know that you are using your time wisely and accomplishing something worthwhile in life. It feels good to make wise decisions rather than living riotously and then feeling condemned because of it. No matter how people may choose to avoid the reality of it, the bottom line is that we feel good when we are doing what we know we should be doing and we feel bad when we don't. The world is filled with people who make wrong decisions and then, when they don't like the result of the choices they have made, they find a way to blame their unfulfilled life on someone or something else. They may medicate or numb their dissatisfaction in some way, but it will always return again and again to renew their misery.

However, even if you feel that you have wasted a lot of your life, all is not lost! Anyone can make a choice and change the direction he or she has been taking in life. We can all start today making

> *Every good and right decision that we make helps overturn the results of the bad ones.*

right choices in line with God's will for our life. Every good and right decision that we make helps overturn the results of the bad ones. God's will always produces good results, so you can get started immediately turning your life around for the better.

Boundaries

When God's Word instructs us to order our conduct and conversation in the will of God (see Psalm 119:1), it means that we must have boundaries. A boundary is similar to a fence you might put around your property. You do it so intruders cannot come in. You are safe within the borders of your fence. We need boundaries in many areas of our lives because they provide peace and safety.

> *He makes peace in your borders; He fills you with the finest of the wheat.*
>
> Psalm 147:14 (AMPC)

A couple I know who have been married for thirty-three years recently shared with me that God revealed to them through this scripture that if they would maintain wise and right boundaries and borders in their married life that they would always have peace. They spent time together praying and seeking God about what those boundaries should be, and He led them to do several things. Decisions were made about their finances, family time, prayer, Bible study, time spent together as a couple, and many other things. They have honored those boundaries, and their testimony is that they have enjoyed the peace of God over the years. That doesn't mean that they have not faced any difficulties, because they certainly have, but God has honored His promise to bless them with peace.

If we set Spirit-led boundaries, then our enemy the devil cannot break through and rob us of the life God intends for us to have.

We need boundaries on our eating and on all things concerning our health. We need them on the financial areas of life, as well as relationships, and work and play. If we have no boundaries we always become excessive in one direction or another.

Spend time with God and come up with a plan of what you desire to accomplish in life and set boundaries that will help you accomplish it. If you want to have great family relationships, then you will need to spend time with your family and be the type of person they enjoy being with. If you want to be financially sound, you will need to work and save money as well as spend it. If you want to be healthy and energetic, you will need to eat properly, get sufficient exercise, and avoid excess stress and other health-related issues. If you want to live in a home that is neat and orderly, then you will have to work to keep it that way. *Nothing good happens accidently.*

Nothing good happens accidently.

Good things occur as we make choices that promote good results. Living life "on purpose" is actually very exciting! It gives us a feeling of being a disciplined person, and we all like that feeling. When we make good decisions, it gives us the joy of partnering with God in having the best life we possibly can have. Take charge of your life under the leadership of the Holy Spirit and start enjoying every day of your new powerful, focused, and fruitful life.

Chapter Summary

- We can spend our lives wishing, but wishing won't change anything. You have to take charge of your life.
- The sooner you make a change, the sooner you will be living the life you truly want to live.
- Taking charge of your life means choosing to do the difficult thing because you are interested in having a good end result.
- Seizing the day is all about making the best choices possible each day of your life.
- Discipline doesn't seem joyful immediately, but it will produce the peace of right living in due time.
- When we make good decisions, it gives us the joy of partnering with God in having the best life we possibly can have.

As I thought about my final comments for this book, the second-to-the-last verse in Ecclesiastes came to mind. Solomon had made choices and tried many different things in life, and not all of them were good. In this book of the Bible, he is giving advice to us, and much of it has been gained by costly and painful experience. I think it is wise to listen to those who have gone before us and have learned by experience the right and wrong choices to make.

> All has been heard; the end of the matter is: Fear God [revere and worship Him, knowing that He is] and keep His commandments, for this is the whole of man [the full, original purpose of his creation, the object of God's providence, the root of character, the foundation of all happiness, the adjustment of all inharmonious circumstances and conditions under the sun] and the whole [duty] for every man.
>
> Ecclesiastes 12:13

This verse of Scripture can be very impactful if you take your time and digest it slowly, meditating on each part thoroughly. So I think my final comment is a paraphrase of what Solomon said. The end of the matter and the conclusion of all that I have written is this: Live your life "on purpose" for a purpose, and with God's help, use the free will He has given you to choose His will! As you do so, it will honor Him greatly, and you will enjoy a satisfying reward!

NOTES

1 http://www.goodreads.com/quotes/437424-god-created-things-which-had
-free-will-that-means-creatures.
2 F. B. Meyer, *The Secret of Guidance*, Fleming H. Revell Company, p. 23.
3 Andrew Murray, *God's Will: Our Dwelling Place*, p. 9.
4 Kent Crockett, *Making Today Count for Eternity*, Multnomah Books, pp. 66–67.
5 http://dailychristianquote.com/tag/choice/.
6 http://www.sermonillustrations.com/a-z/d/decision.htm.
7 http://www.brainyquote.com/quotes/quotes/n/nickvujici632096.html.
8 Brainyquote.com.
9 http://www.goodreads.com/author/quotes/102203.Corrie_ten_Boom.
10 http://www.brainyquote.com/quotes/quotes/l/leonardoda120920.html.
11 http://www.goodreads.com/quotes/44552-yesterday-is-gone-tomorrow
-has-not-yet-come-we-have.
12 http://www.brainyquote.com/quotes/quotes/w/winstonchu101477.html.
13 http://webstersdictionary1828.com/Dictionary/interrupt.
14 http://thinkexist.com/quotation/by_prevailing_over_all_obstacles_and
_distractions/171483.html.
15 http://www.nytimes.com/2013/05/05/opinion/sunday/a-focus-on
-distraction.html?_r=0.
16 http://www.brainyquote.com/quotes/quotes/b/benjaminfr109062.html.
17 http://www.goodreads.com/quotes/64541-the-purpose-of-life-is-not-to
-be-happy-it.
18 http://www.sermonillustrations.com/a-z/p/purpose.htm.
19 http://www.merriam-webster.com/dictionary/passion.
20 *Webster's American 1828 Dictionary*.
21 http://www.goodreads.com/quotes/824273-so-much-attention-is-paid
-to-the-aggressive-sins-such.
22 http://www.goodreads.com/quotes/548342-silence-in-the-face-of-evil-is
-itself-evil-god.
23 http://www.family-times.net/illustration/Desire/201015/.

24 George Barna and David Burton, *U-Turn: Restoring America to the Strength of Its Roots.*

25 http://www.sermoncentral.com/illustrations/sermon-illustration-ronald-thorington-stories-64514.asp.

26 *More of the Best of Bits & Pieces*, p. 73.

27 http://daringtolivefully.com/goal-quotes.

28 http://techcrunch.com/2011/10/06/jobs-focus-is-about-saying-no/.

29 http://www.brainyquote.com/quotes/quotes/h/harperlee119674.html.

30 http://www.goodreads.com/quotes/88934-do-not-have-your-concert-first-and-then-tune-your.

31 http://www.goodreads.com/quotes/26920-you-will-never-find-time-for-anything-if-you-want.

Do you have a real relationship with Jesus?

God loves you! He created you to be a special, unique, one-of-a-kind individual, and He has a specific purpose and plan for your life. And through a personal relationship with your Creator—God—you can discover a way of life that will truly satisfy your soul.

No matter who you are, what you've done, or where you are in your life right now, God's love and grace are greater than your sin—your mistakes. Jesus willingly gave His life so you can receive forgiveness from God and have new life in Him. He's just waiting for you to invite Him to be your Savior and Lord.

If you are ready to commit your life to Jesus and follow Him, all you have to do is ask Him to forgive your sins and give you a fresh start in the life you are meant to live. Begin by praying this prayer…

Lord Jesus, thank You for giving Your life for me and forgiving me of my sins so I can have a personal relationship with You. I am sincerely sorry for the mistakes I've made, and I know I need You to help me live right.

Your Word says in Romans 10:9, "If you declare with your mouth, 'Jesus is Lord,' and believe in your heart that God raised him from the dead, you will be saved" (NIV). I believe You are the Son of God and confess You as my Savior and Lord. Take me just as I am, and work in my heart, making me the person You want me to be. I want to live for You, Jesus, and I am so grateful that You are giving me a fresh start in my new life with You today.

I love You, Jesus!

It's so amazing to know that God loves us so much! He wants to have a deep, intimate relationship with us that grows every day as we spend time with Him in prayer and Bible study. And we want to encourage you in your new life in Christ.

Please visit joycemeyer.org/salvation to request Joyce's book *A New Way of Living*, which is our gift to you. We also have other free resources online to help you make progress in pursuing everything God has for you.

Congratulations on your fresh start in your life in Christ! We hope to hear from you soon.

JOYCE MEYER is one of the world's leading practical Bible teachers. Her daily broadcast, *Enjoying Everyday Life*, airs on hundreds of television networks and radio stations worldwide.

Joyce has written more than 100 inspirational books. Her bestsellers include *Power Thoughts*; *The Confident Woman*; *Look Great, Feel Great*; *Starting Your Day Right*; *Ending Your Day Right*; *Approval Addiction*; *How to Hear from God*; *Beauty for Ashes*; and *Battlefield of the Mind*.

Joyce travels extensively, holding conferences throughout the year and speaking to thousands around the world.

Joyce Meyer Ministries
P.O. Box 655
Fenton, MO 63026
USA
(636) 349-0303

Joyce Meyer Ministries—Canada
P.O. Box 7700
Vancouver, BC V6B 4E2
Canada
(800) 868-1002

Joyce Meyer Ministries—Australia
Locked Bag 77
Mansfield Delivery Centre
Queensland 4122
Australia
(07) 3349 1200

Joyce Meyer Ministries—England
P.O. Box 1549
Windsor SL4 1GT
United Kingdom
01753 831102

Joyce Meyer Ministries—South Africa
P.O. Box 5
Cape Town 8000
South Africa
(27) 21-701-1056

The Penny
Perfect Love (previously published as *God Is Not Mad at You*)*
The Power of Being Positive
The Power of Being Thankful
The Power of Determination
The Power of Forgiveness
The Power of Simple Prayer
Power Thoughts
Power Thoughts Devotional
Reduce Me to Love
The Secret Power of Speaking God's Word
The Secrets of Spiritual Power
The Secret to True Happiness
Seven Things That Steal Your Joy
Start Your New Life Today
Starting Your Day Right
Straight Talk
Teenagers Are People Too!
Trusting God Day by Day
The Word, the Name, the Blood
Unshakeable Trust
Woman to Woman
You Can Begin Again

JOYCE MEYER SPANISH TITLES

Belleza en Lugar de Cenizas (Beauty for Ashes)
Buena Salud, Buena Vida (Good Health, Good Life)
Cambia Tus Palabras, Cambia Tu Vida (Change Your Words, Change Your Life)
El Campo de Batalla de la Mente (Battlefield of the Mind)
Como Formar Buenos Habitos y Romper Malos Habitos (Making Good Habits, Breaking Bad Habits)
La Conexión de la Mente (The Mind Connection)
Confianza inquebrantable (Unshakeable Trust)
Dios No Está Enojado Contigo (God Is Not Mad at You)
La Dosis de Aprobación (The Approval Fix)
Empezando Tu Día Bien (Starting Your Day Right)
Hazte Un Favor a Ti Mismo...Perdona (Do Yourself a Favor...Forgive)
Madre Segura de sí Misma (The Confident Mom)
Pensamientos de Poder (Power Thoughts)
*Sobrecarga (Overload)**
Termina Bien tu Día (Ending Your Day Right)
Usted Puede Comenzar de Nuevo (You Can Begin Again)
Viva Valientemente (Living Courageously)

* Study Guide available for this title

BOOKS BY DAVE MEYER

Life Lines